Advanced praise for *Raising Vegan Children in a Non-Vegan World*:

"To raise a child as a vegan in this very non-vegan world is an act of courage, principle and compassion. It takes a writer with those qualities, like Erin Pavlina, to create the ultimate guide to this extremely challenging task of *Raising Vegan Children in a Non-Vegan World*. I commend her for her love of life, her dedication, and her creative efforts, and I recommend this book most highly. It gifts us with a beautiful vision and is a pathway to a saner, healthier future for us all."

Michael Klaper, M.D., Author
***Vegan Nutrition: Pure and Simple*;**
Pregnancy, Children, and the Vegan Diet

"Raising children who eat, think, and live differently than their peers and the society around them can be a daunting task. This book offers a host of useful and creative ideas for bringing up healthy, self-confident, and compassionate children."

Deo Robbins, Co-founder
***EarthSave International*, and grandmother of twins**

"*Raising Vegan Children in a Non-Vegan World* is a comprehensive resource for vegan families. Real-life tested, this book is written by a vegan mom who draws on extensive interviews with hundreds of other vegan parents. Indispensable for vegan families, *Raising Vegan Children in a Non-Vegan World* is filled with in-depth information, practical tips and helpful suggestions for every situation."

Peggy O'Mara, Editor and Publisher
***Mothering* magazine**

"This book supplies detailed answers to the really hard questions. It goes beyond the basics to help parents successfully navigate life as vegans in any stage of parenting. Indispensable!"

Melanie Wilson, Editor-in-Chief
***Vegetarian Baby and Child* magazine**

Raising Vegan Children In a Non-Vegan World

A Complete Guide for Parents

Erin Pavlina

VEGFAMILY
Los Angeles, California
www.vegfamily.com

Published by:
VegFamily
P.O. Box 571961
Tarzana, CA 91357-1961
www.vegfamily.com

Cover Design: Cathi Stevenson
Artwork Provided by: www.ArtToday.com

ISBN: 0-9725102-0-6
Library of Congress Control Number: 2002114053

Printed in the United States of America

10 9 8 7 6 5 4 3 2 1

Contents

Disclaimer

This book was designed to provide information about the subject matter covered. It is sold with the understanding that the publisher and authors are not engaged in rendering medical, legal, or other professional advice. If medical or legal assistance is required, the services of a competent professional should be sought.

Every effort has been made to make this book as complete and accurate as possible. However, there may be mistakes both typographical and in content. Therefore, this text should be used only as a general guide and not as the ultimate source of vegan parenting information. Furthermore, this book contains information regarding how to raise vegan children only up to the time of printing.

The purpose of this manual is to educate and entertain. The authors and VegFamily shall have neither liability nor responsibility to any person or entity with respect to any loss or damage caused or alleged to be caused directly or indirectly by the information contained in this book.

If you do not wish to be bound by the above, you may return this book in new condition to the publisher for a full refund.

Acknowledgements

Writing this book was a thrilling experience. I'm grateful to many people for their input, advice, and encouragement.

I am deeply grateful to Steve Pavlina, my husband, dearest love, and best friend, who asked me one day, "What would you do if you knew you couldn't fail?" This book is the beginning of my answer. I am continually guided by his wisdom, intelligence, and example. To my daughter, Emily, for being my inspiration.

Heartfelt thanks go to Michael Klaper, Peggy O'Mara, Deo Robbins, Joanne Stepaniak, Brenda Davis, Melanie Wilson, Susan Weingartner, Kerrie Saunders, Dennis Bayomi, Ellie Callahan, and Lauren Feder. They each read the entire manuscript or selected chapters and reviewed them for quality and accuracy. Thank you all for holding my hand and honoring me with your wisdom.

Special thanks to Allison Rivers, for her support, friendship, and encouragement every step of the way. Her contribution to this book, and to my life, are immeasurable.

A big thank you to my editor, Rebecca Nyberg, who came to my rescue, and put the polish on this book.

A final thank you goes to the vegan parents who contributed their time, stories, wisdom, experience, and information to this project. Without them this book just wouldn't be complete.

Preface

It was a brisk September morning in 1999. Thirteen weeks into my vegan pregnancy, I was surfing the Internet trying to find information about how to raise a vegan child. I found tidbits on one Web site, a mention on another, and a lot of information about how to raise a *vegetarian* child, but nothing specifically related to raising *vegan* children. I was frustrated. I knew I couldn't be the only person planning to raise a vegan child, and I desperately wanted to connect with other vegan parents so I could find out how they were raising their children.

Since there was such a lack of information on this subject, and because I was a Web developer by trade, I decided to create a Web site specifically for vegan parents. In October of 1999, I launched VegFamily, an online magazine for vegan parents. I had 63 visitors my first month, and I was elated to have found so many people raising vegan children. I set up a discussion board so we could all share our experiences and information, and I continued to add fresh content to the Web site. Search engines and word of mouth began driving a great deal of traffic to my Web site, and within a year VegFamily was drawing 3,000 visitors per month. I found myself fielding hundreds of emails each month from parents who wanted to know how to raise vegan children. I gathered a group of experts from the vegan community to help me answer all of these questions, but there were far more questions than they could handle.

By January 2002, VegFamily was getting more than 15,000 visitors per month, and boasted one of the largest collections of articles and information about raising vegan children anywhere on the Internet. My email inbox was bursting with comments, questions, and correspondence from vegan and vegetarian parents all over the world. I realized that I was answering many of the same questions repeatedly. People all wanted the same information, and someone needed to compile it into one, comprehensive resource.

In May 2002, I began outlining a book that would explain how to raise a vegan child in a non-vegan world. I interviewed and spoke with hundreds of vegan parents. I drew upon their experiences, and my own, and I consulted with experts in medicine and vegan nutrition. Interspersed throughout the book, you'll find tips and advice from many of the parents whom I interviewed.

After years of running VegFamily, and meeting and speaking with thousands of other parents, I now have the certainty I was seeking back in 1999. My hope is that this book will allay any fears or concerns you have about raising vegan children, and that it will give you the confidence you need to successfully raise happy, healthy vegan children in a non-vegan world.

Erin Pavlina
President
VegFamily

Chapter 1

BEING VEGAN

What does it mean to be a vegan? Is it a diet or a lifestyle? Why do people decide to become vegans? What do vegans eat and wear, and what products do they buy? Is honey vegan? How do you know if a food has animal products in it? What should you do with your non-vegan clothing, furniture, and jewelry? How do decide if you should take your kids to the zoo and if you should let them have pony rides?

If you're new to veganism, this chapter will serve as a guide to understanding the vegan lifestyle. If you're already a vegan, you probably know the answers to most of these questions. In any case, this chapter will attempt to answer all of those questions for you.

Definition of Veganism
A vegan (pronounced VEE'gun) is someone who avoids using or consuming animal products. Vegans don't eat meat such as beef, chicken, fish, pork, turkey, snails, frog legs, etc. Vegans also don't eat dairy products which includes milk, butter, eggs, cheese, sour cream, yogurt, and cottage cheese. In addition, vegans don't eat foods of animal origin, such as honey, gelatin, casein, whey, or rennet. Vegans avoid wearing clothing that was made from animal products like

fur, silk, or leather. In their daily lives and in their households, vegans avoid using products, cleaners, and toiletries that contain animal ingredients or that were tested on animals. Vegans tend to avoid amusements where animals are used, held captive, or mistreated, such as zoos, marine parks, rodeos, and circuses. In general, vegans take a compassionate look at all aspects of their lives, and try to improve the conditions of humans, animals and the environment.

Reasons for Going Vegan

There are many reasons why a person might choose to go vegan. The three most common reasons are to help the animals, to protect the environment, and to improve one's health. How are these three areas improved by going vegan?

Helping the animals. Food animals are treated abominably. They live in cramped cages, are forced to endure physical and psychological hardships, are injected with drugs, sprayed with chemicals, fed things they have no business eating, and live short, terror-filled lives. When you stop eating food animals you stop contributing to their suffering.

If you think that eating eggs doesn't harm a chicken, think again. Laying hens aren't sitting on a nest in the tropics sipping iced tea and dropping eggs whenever they feel like it. They're packed into small cages with other chickens, barely able to move. Their sensitive beaks are crudely trimmed or sliced off so that they don't cause injuries or peck one another to death. They are forced to lay far beyond their natural capacities. They're injected with antibiotics, drugs, and hormones. Eating the feces of other chickens is not uncommon, since the cages and the food are littered with excrement. If you think the life of a hen is bad, wait until you learn what happens to the chickens who are born male! Male chicks are often discarded at birth. By discarded, I mean thrown into a trash bag with other baby chicks and sent to the incinerator. If they're "lucky" and suffocate first they don't have to feel the horrific pain of being burned to death.

What about drinking milk? Doesn't the farmer take care of the cow and milk her every morning by hand? Hardly. Dairy cows are tied in stalls, unable to turn around. They are injected with hormones. A machine hooked to the cow's delicate udders milks her whether she's ready or not. She never gets a chance to feed her babies, since they are taken away from her at birth. A cow who would normally live 20 to 25 years, lives perhaps five to seven years in these conditions.

When you stop eating animals, you have the right to sleep better at night. But that's just the beginning!

Protecting the environment. Animal agriculture uses up vital food resources that could be used to feed the millions of children who are starving to death each year. Feed for farm animals requires a lot of land, water, and fertilizer, and could be used to feed the human population directly. Cattle grazing causes topsoil erosion, which means the land is less capable of producing crops. Animal waste products are dumped into lagoons and on land, which pollutes our waters and environment. We lose trees, we lose rainforest, and we lose oxygen. We bring about the extinction of animals living in the rainforest, and we're altering our ecosystem.

But vegans are sustained on far less land than omnivores. Twenty thousand pounds of potatoes can be grown on the same amount of land required to make 165 pounds of beef. It takes three-and-a-half acres of land each year to feed an omnivore, but only one sixth of an acre to feed a vegan.

When you go vegan you stop contributing to the degradation of our planet's resources and you help protect our environment.

Improving health. Vegans suffer fewer health problems than do people who eat meat. For example, a vegan is less likely to suffer from cancer, heart disease, heart attack, high cholesterol, obesity, diabetes, high blood pressure, stroke, gallstones, diverticular disease, and food-borne illnesses. Vegan foods contain zero cholesterol, they're high in fiber, they're water-rich, and they contain fewer harmful chemicals than meat and dairy products. Vegans live longer, feel better, and suffer less than people who eat meat. Who wouldn't want that?

Food

People accustomed to eating meat and dairy products often have a hard time fathoming what vegans eat. I've been asked: "If you don't eat meat, where will you get your protein?" "No meat or dairy? What's left?" and "How can you live without cheese?" Be assured that you will neither starve nor suffer eating a vegan diet. You'll be eating from the following food groups: fruits, vegetables, grains, nuts, legumes, and seeds.

In recent years, there's been a movement in the vegan community to create a new food guide to replace the outdated Four Food Groups originally created by the dairy industry. I've seen several new guides appear and, although they differ slightly, they all have the same basic information. The Physicians Committee for Responsible Medicine (PCRM) has formulated a New Four Foods Group that is very easy to understand and follow. However, a more detailed Food Pyramid was designed especially for vegans by Brenda Davis, R.D. and Vesanto Melina, M.S., R.D. in their book *Becoming Vegan*. What follows is a synopsis of those two systems.

Whole grains. PCRM recommends 5 or more servings per day, while *Becoming Vegan* recommends 6-11 servings per day. Foods in this category include bread, pasta, rice, cereal, barley, millet, oats, tortillas, and corn.

A serving size is defined as one slice of bread, ½ cup hot cereal, one ounce of dry cereal, or ½ cup cooked grains.

Although the recommendations seem to differ significantly, both suggest that you should be getting a large portion of your daily servings from the whole grains group.

Vegetables. Both the PCRM and *Becoming Vegan* recommend 3 or more servings of vegetables each day. Dark green leafy vegetables such as broccoli, collards, kale, spinach, and bok choy are excellent sources of key nutrients like vitamin C, beta-carotene, riboflavin, iron, calcium, and fiber. Also, dark yellow and orange vegetables such as pumpkin, carrots, sweet potatoes, and squash are excellent sources of beta-carotene. Be sure to include a wide variety of vegetables in your diet, and try to get at least one serving of raw vegetables each day. Salads are good opportunities to include raw vegetables such as lettuce, carrots, cucumber, and broccoli.

A serving size is defined as 1 cup of raw vegetables, ½ cup cooked vegetables, or ¾ cup vegetable juice.

Fruits. PCRM recommends 3 or more servings per day, while *Becoming Vegan* suggests that 2 or more servings per day be consumed. Fruits are high in fiber, vitamin C, and beta-carotene. Fruits highest in vitamin C include strawberries, citrus fruits, cantaloupe, mangos, and papayas.

A serving size is defined as one medium apple, banana, or orange, or ½ cup cooked fruit, 4 ounces of fruit juice, or ¼ cup dried fruit. Avoid bottled fruit juice that is refined and less nutritive. Drink fresh fruit juice whenever possible.

Legumes. The PCRM recommends 2 or more servings per day, while *Becoming Vegan* recommends 2-3 servings. Foods in this category include split peas, lentils, beans, tofu, tempeh, chickpeas, soymilk, nuts, and seeds. Note that nuts and seeds are excellent sources of vitamin E and minerals. Eating foods in this category along with foods high in vitamin C will help increase iron absorption.

A serving size is defined as 1 cup cooked legumes (beans, lentils, dried peas), ½ cup tofu or tempeh, 8 ounces of soymilk, 2-3 slices of veggie deli "meats," or 3 tablespoons of nut or seed butters.

Calcium. *Becoming Vegan* includes a special category for calcium. The recommendation for this mineral is 6 – 8 servings per day. Examples of foods in this group, along with their serving sizes, are: ½ cup fortified soymilk, ¼ cup calcium-set tofu, ½ cup calcium-fortified orange juice, ¼ cup almonds, 3 tablespoons almond butter, 1 cup cooked green vegetables (kale, collards, broccoli, okra) or 2 cups raw green vegetables, 1 cup high-calcium beans (soy, navy, white, black, turtle), ¼ cup dry hijiki seaweed, 1 tablespoon blackstrap molasses, or 5 figs.

Other essentials. *Becoming Vegan* also makes mention of three essential categories that the PCRM does not: omega-3 fatty acids, vitamin B_{12}, and vitamin D. A great source of plant-based omega-3 fatty acids is flax oil. Red Star Vegetarian Support Formula nutritional yeast is a good source of B_{12}. Get vitamin D from sunlight exposure, or from D_2 supplements. We'll discuss these nutrients in more detail in chapter 4.

If you're new to veganism, you may want to refer to these guidelines often until you get used to incorporating all of these items into your daily meals. Rest assured, in time you won't need to refer to charts and pyramids; you'll know intuitively if you're getting enough servings from each category.

Real Stories from Real Parents:
When asked what the term "vegan" means, our 3-year-old Marcella said, "It means I can eat it!" – Kerrie

---

Hidden Animal Ingredients
Now that you know what foods are vegan, you need to know what foods aren't vegan. Besides the obvious foods like

meat, butter, eggs, and cheese, there are a few other animal products lurking around. Following is a list of the most common hidden animal ingredients.

Gelatin. Gelatin is a protein made by boiling the skin, tendons, ligaments, and/or bones of animals in water. It is often found in puddings, fruit gelatins, marshmallows, cosmetics, and candies, and it is sometimes used in wine-making. Gelatin is often used in medicines and supplement capsules.

Honey. Bees make honey by collecting nectar from flowers and then regurgitating it back and forth between them until it is partially digested. In the final stage, bees fan the honey until it becomes cool and thick. This is when humans harvest the honey. Beekeepers cause harm to the bees when harvesting the honey. The official position of The Vegan Society in England prohibits vegans from eating honey. Also note that neither beeswax nor honeycomb are vegan.

Whey. Whey is the watery liquid from cow's milk that is left behind after most of the protein solids have been removed, as in cheese-making. Whey has found its way into a vast array of prepared foods. Cake mixes, protein powders, candies, cookies, breads, salad dressings, and many other processed foods use whey because it's a cheap ingredient. Be sure to check labels carefully, as whey has been insinuated into many products that were formerly vegan.

Casein. Casein is a protein that is found in cow's milk. It is often found in products designed for people who are lactose intolerant. Be especially wary of soy cheeses because many of them will have casein or caseinate in them!

Lactic Acid. Lactic acid is found in the blood and muscle tissue of animals. However, for most commercial purposes lactic acid is made from the fermentation of hydrolyzed cornstarch or beet sugar. In some forms there may be a synthetic component, or the fermentation medium may include whey from cow's milk. When you see lactic acid listed on a product, it may or may not be from an animal. You'll have to contact the company to find out which form they use.

Lactose. This is one of the sugars found in animal milk. It is a common ingredient in many prepared foods.

Lanolin. A product of the oil glands of sheep, extracted from their wool. Lanolin is often found in lotions, cosmetics, and creams.

Lecithin. Lecithin can be derived from animal or plant sources. If you see soy lecithin on a package, it's vegan. Otherwise, question the company.

Oleic Acid. Oleic acid can be made from animal or vegetable oils and fats, and is commonly found in foods, soaps, lipstick, and many other skin preparations.

Rennet. Rennet is an enzyme found in the lining of calves' stomachs and is commonly used to make cheese. Avoid products made with rennet.

Royal Jelly. Royal jelly is a secretion from the throat glands of worker honeybees. It is fed to the larvae in a colony and to all queen larvae.

Stearic Acid. This fat is most often taken from the stomach of pigs. It is used in a number of foods, supplements, and personal care items.

For a complete list of animal ingredients and a list of foods that often contain these hidden ingredients, see www.vegfamily.com/lists/animal-ingredients.htm.

Personal Care Products

Ever read the ingredients on your shampoo, conditioner, or soap? First, you'll probably notice many chemical ingredients with names that are hard to pronounce. What you may not know is that some of the chemical ingredients were derived from animals. Also, many companies test their products on animals to ensure that they won't harm the human eye or be harmful if swallowed. What does that mean for you? It means you'll have to make an initial effort to find some vegan products, and then stop using the ones that contain animal ingredients or that were tested on animals. Luckily, there are hundreds of companies opting to make their products without animal ingredients and without animal testing. For a list of companies that make cruelty-free products, see www.vegfamily.com/lists/cruelty-free-companies.htm.

How do you know if the products you're currently using contain animal ingredients or were tested on animals? You should contact the company and ask them. Look for the company's phone number or web address on the package. Ask whether their product is free of animal ingredients and whether it is tested on animals.

Look closely for hidden animal ingredients on products such as shampoo, conditioner, hair gel, hair mousse, hair spray, lotion, cosmetics, nail polish, perfume, lip balm, soap, toothpaste, deodorant, and shaving cream. On the bright side, once you find vegan products you like, it's just as easy to buy vegan as it was to buy non-vegan versions.

Jewelry, Clothing, and Furniture

Being vegan doesn't stop with giving up steak and switching shampoo. Start looking around your environment and see what else you own that was made from animal products.

Jewelry. Many people don't realize that their jewelry may be made from animal products. If you own jewelry made with any of the following items you may want to find replacements for them: ivory, pearl, tortoiseshell (hairclips or glasses frames), leather, or bone.

Clothing. Open your closet and take a good look at what's in there. Do you own anything made of leather, silk, fur, wool, angora, snakeskin, alligator skin, rawhide, camel hair, or feathers? Don't forget to check your shoes and purses too.

Furniture. Is your couch leather? Is your bedspread made of goose down? What about your pillow? If you can't afford to replace the items, use them up and don't buy them again.

Household Cleaners

Now that you've cleaned out your refrigerator, pantry, closet, bathroom, and jewelry box, and you've given your furniture the once-over, it's time to get cleaning. But wait, what's in your cleaning products? Many contain non-vegan ingredients. Pull out everything you've got and start reading labels. If all you see are chemicals you can't pronounce, check them against the animal ingredient list at www.vegfamily.com/lists/animal-ingredients.htm. If you can't find it on the list, call the company and ask if their product contains animal ingredients. If they don't know (very common), use up the product and start buying new products from companies who make vegan household cleaning products. Go to www.vegfamily.com/lists/cruelty-free-companies.htm for a list. Remember that once you find vegan versions it's easy to keep buying from the same companies.

What to do With Non-Vegan Items

What should you do once you find all these non-vegan items lurking in your home? Select the option below that makes you feel the most comfortable.

Sell them. Consider selling your non-vegan items (i.e., couches, clothing, and jewelry) at a yard sale. Then use the money to buy vegan replacements, or give the money to an animal rights organization. Get your kids into the act too. For everything they sell, let them use the money to buy something for themselves, or let them choose an organization to donate the money to.

Donate them. Many people donate their non-vegan clothing and jewelry to homeless and women's shelters. You can also donate soap and other unopened toiletry items. That's better than throwing them away.

Use them up. Some people don't have the financial means to part with their non-vegan items. In that case, continue to use them, but select vegan versions when it's time to buy new ones. Also, if you have a little bit of shampoo, conditioner, nail polish, or makeup remaining, you can use it up so it doesn't go to waste. Just buy a vegan version next time. There's no point in wasting an item that you've already bought.

Throw them away. If the item is of no use to anyone or you simply don't want anyone else to have it, throw it away and start from scratch. If you're thinking about throwing away something that's in good condition, please consider donating it to a needy person or organization instead.

Vegan Ethics

After I read *Diet for a New America* by John Robbins, I had a paradigm shift. I realized that being vegan isn't just about eating differently, it's about living differently. It's about making different decisions, some of them difficult. It's about taking the compassionate route even when it means standing alone or being singled out. Vegan ethics are as much a part of being vegan as avoiding meat and dairy products. Here are some questions to think about.

Will you take your child to the zoo? On a pony ride? To the circus? If your child wants a companion animal, will you get one from the pet store or an animal shelter? Will you spay or neuter animals in your care? Will you let your child have a hamster or bird in a cage?

What will you do when ants invade your home? What about cockroaches, mice or rats? How will you prevent snails and squirrels from eating up your garden?

What about your occupation? Do you work for a company that makes animal products? Do you work for a company that donates money to a cause you don't want to support?

What about your health? Would you take drugs that contain animal ingredients? That were tested on animals? What if your life depended on it? Are you practicing safe sex using non-vegan birth control methods?

Notice that I didn't suggest answers to these questions. When it comes to vegan ethics, you must let your own conscience guide you. Do not let other people, including other vegans, tell you where to stand on the issues. Think about them and make your own decisions. We live in a world that is not wholly vegan. There will be times when you may have to select the option that is the lesser of two evils. Consistently strive to live a compassionate and ethical life. That's all anyone can do.

> For a list of books covering veganism and ethics, see www.vegfamily.com/book-reviews/index.htm.

Chapter 2

HELPING CHILDREN TRANSITION

Raising children vegan from birth will be relatively easy since being vegan is all they will know. However, transitioning children who are accustomed to eating meat and dairy products will be more difficult, especially if they are older. How will you explain to your toddler that she isn't getting the kids' meal at her favorite fast food restaurant? How will you get your teenager to stop using hair sprays that contain animal products? Will your children grasp the concept of being kind to animals?

Then there are the tough questions that your kids may ask: "What happens to animals used for food?" "Why does grandma eat meat if it's so bad?" and "Why can't I have that anymore?"

What happens in mixed marriages when one partner wants to go vegan and raise vegan children, but the other one does not? Is it possible to raise vegan children in a mixed marriage? How do other couples do it?

How will you explain to family and friends that your family has gone vegan? Will they understand, or will they question your decision? What can you do to make it easier for your child to have a play date at a non-vegan friend's house?

By the end of this chapter, you will have answers to all of these questions, and you'll have more confidence in your ability to raise happy, healthy vegan children.

Toddlers
Transitioning toddlers to veganism is great because they still listen to you and count on you for their sustenance. It will be fairly easy to transition a child who is between one and five years old. Here's how to do it.

Explaining veganism to your toddler. How should you explain that the family is going vegan to someone so young? Obviously you don't want to use graphic details of how animals are turned into food, nor do I think it's necessary at this age to tell children that they've been eating dead animals. Instead, you can simply say, "Mommy recently learned that some of the foods we eat are not very healthy, so we're going to be switching to some better foods soon. But don't worry, the new foods will be just as delicious as the ones you're used to."

After your child has been vegan for a while, you can let him know that one of the reasons it's so great to be a vegan is that it's kinder to the animals. You'll have to judge just how many details your child can tolerate.

Adopting a new diet. The key to transitioning your toddler to a vegan diet is to quickly replace the foods that don't matter, and slowly replace the foods that do. For example, replace butter with non-hydrogenated margarine or oil. Bake with soymilk or rice milk instead of cow's milk. Switch to vegan versions of mayonnaise, cream cheese, sour cream, and salad dressings. Serve burritos with beans instead of beef. Try veggie burgers instead of beef burgers. He probably won't notice or care. You can make these modifications overnight, and you probably won't hear a complaint.

For foods like cereal, grilled cheese sandwiches, scrambled eggs, pizza, macaroni and cheese, and chicken nuggets, you'll have to slowly introduce vegan versions into his diet. Find a soymilk he likes for use in cereal; it may take some trial and error. Instead of scrambled eggs, try making scrambled tofu (from scratch or from a mix). It's possible to make a vegan grilled cheese, it just takes a little effort to find a vegan cheese and get it to melt. You can find vegan versions of chicken nuggets in the frozen section of the grocery store, or you can make your own.

Being vegan doesn't mean giving up flavor and taste, it just means finding new favorites. Reassure your child that he will still be eating foods he likes – they just won't contain any animal products.

Instilling a sense of compassion. Toddlers naturally love animals so it will be easy to teach them compassion. Teach your toddler the proper way to care for her companion animals, if she has any, and teach her to be respectful of all animals she may encounter. You can also read stories to your kids about animals or vegetarian children.

Becoming earth-friendly. It's never too early to teach your child how to respect the earth and keep it clean. Show her how to sort the trash, and teach her that recycling is important to the well-being of the planet. You can also teach her not to waste water and other resources. The habits you instill in your child while she's young will carry forward into adulthood.

Young Children

Transitioning children who are between the ages of five and ten will serve up more challenges than transitioning a toddler, but you still have an excellent chance for a smooth ride. Here are some tips to make the transition easy.

Explaining veganism to your young child. Children in this age group can understand the connection between animals and food, but you still don't want to be too graphic. Explain to your child that animals are treated very poorly and are eventually sold to supermarkets where people end up buying and eating them. He may even be grossed out by this concept, but that's acceptable. After you tell him what happens to food animals, say, "But we're going to stop eating animals because we don't think it's very nice. We also found out that it isn't very healthy to eat animals, so we want to start eating some foods that will make our bodies healthier. You may even get fewer colds and sore throats, and you probably won't have as many tummy aches either." Likely he'll have some questions for you, especially about why you ate animals before and why his friends and relatives still eat them. You'll learn how to answer those questions later in this chapter.

Adopting a new diet. Children may be attached to their favorite foods, so adopting a new diet is going to be a little tougher than if they were toddlers. Start slowly by replacing the things that don't matter so much. Buy non-hydrogenated margarine instead of butter, vegan cream cheese instead of regular cream cheese, veggie burgers instead of beef burgers, and vegan salad dressings and mayonnaise instead of the non-vegan versions. Let your child get used to these new foods before you take the next step.

Next, introduce him to new foods without taking away his old ones. Let him try scrambled tofu, soymilk, veggie bacon, pizza with vegan cheese (or without any cheese at all), veggie deli slices, lasagna with tofu cheese instead of ricotta, spaghetti with veggie meatballs, and vegan versions of cookies and ice cream. Once he is comfortable with the new foods, and is eating them more often than the old ones, you can stop buying the old foods and stick with the new. In no time he'll have left the non-vegan foods behind and will be happily eating the new foods.

Instilling a sense of compassion. Kids in this age group love animals. If you don't already have a companion animal, consider getting one from a shelter. Be sure to prepare your child well so she'll know how to take care of it properly. Let the animal become part of the family. Remind her of how special it is to be a vegan, and of how grateful the animals are to her for being a vegan. Also, look for books that she can read, or that you can read to her, that exemplify vegan values.

Being earth-friendly. Make sure that your child knows how to recycle, and that she understands how to conserve resources and energy. Let her collect newspapers or aluminum cans, recycle them, and spend the money she earns on something special for herself. Help her plant a garden or teach her how to take care of plants. Let her know how her food choices affect the planet. Make it educational and fun!

Real Stories from Real Parents:
Don't underestimate your child's power of comprehension, and don't shield him or her from the realities that these animals face in order to feed an overindulged society. Explain how people are starving in the world as meat-based societies abuse resources to satisfy their urge for flesh. Explain that the planet and all its inhabitants could live healthy lives if this diet were implemented. Explain how it all begins with one person. – Danielle

---

Pre-Teens and Young Teens
Children between the ages of 11 and 15 may be a hard group to transition. Their habits are fairly well ingrained, they know what they like to eat, and they're looking for any reason to say "no" to you. To successfully transition children at this age you may need to get leverage; don't just tell them how horrible it is to eat meat, *show* them.

Explaining veganism to your young teen. Let your young teen know how animals are raised and slaughtered, but don't be any more graphic than you feel is necessary. Get him to see the connection between what he eats and where that food comes from by telling him verbally or using books, literature, pictures, or videos.

If you have a sensitive child, there's no need to be explicit. Many children this age transition easily after you explain that hamburger is really a dead cow, bacon comes from a dead pig, and chicken nuggets contain pieces of the chicken.

To find videos, literature, and books that explain the connection between food and animals, visit www.peta.com, www.earthsave.org, and www.veganoutreach.org.

Don't forget to mention the health aspects of going vegan, which are covered fully in chapter 3.

Adopting a new diet. As with other age groups, transitioning your young teen to a new diet is going to take some preparation and patience. Be sure to have a good collection of vegan cookbooks in the house. Let everyone in the family pick out recipes that seem interesting, go shopping together, and get cooking. Make it an adventure! Let each member of the family rate the recipe on a scale of one to ten. Keep trying out new recipes until you have a collection of at least 20 favorite family recipes, and make those often. For help in handling birthday parties, special events, and social situations, see chapter 6.

Instilling a sense of compassion. Find ways to show your child how beautiful animals are when they are allowed to live in peace. Take her to nature trails and show her animals living in their natural habitats. Rent movies like *Babe* and *Chicken Run* that showcase how animals are treated and how truly loving they are. Give her *Charlotte's Web* and other books that show how wonderful and smart animals are. Teach her to look out for the animals in the neighborhood, and if you're able, rescue some strays.

Being earth-friendly. Help your child find projects in school that show classmates how to conserve resources, recycle, and keep the environment healthy. Teach him to reuse items he owns and to refrain from wasting. Find creative ways to help the environment as a family. Show your child how proud you are that he is making a difference.

Teenagers
Teenagers are sometimes the most difficult group to transition, but sometimes they are the easiest. In fact, often it's teenagers who decide to go vegan first and then get their parents to make the transition. If your teen is the one leading you, excellent! If, on the other hand, you've decided to go vegan and your teen is less than enthusiastic about joining you, be prepared for disappointment. Once a child reaches the age of 16 to 18, the amount of influence you have on her dwindles. Here's what you need to know to maximize your chances of successfully transitioning your teenager.

Tell your teen why you're going vegan. First, tell your teen why you've decided to go vegan. Tell her what you know about how animals are treated, how eating animal products damage health, and that eating animal products impacts the environment. If she wants to know more, tell her what your plan is for going vegan. If she doesn't seem interested, don't push.

Go on about your business. If your teen isn't interested in what you're doing, just go vegan without him. Be an example. In time, your teen may notice your improved health or how happy you seem to be eating tofu scramble. Be enthusiastic about what you're doing, but don't be preachy.

Replace what you can, leave the rest. If you walk into your teen's room and demand that she hand over all her cosmetics and hair spray, you're going to have one angry teen! First, replace what you can, the household cleaners and detergents, for example. Also, start stocking the refrigerator and freezer with vegan foods and meals, and let your teen have access to them.

What to do if your teen is interested in going vegan. If your teen is interested in going vegan, help her understand all the facets of veganism; her diet, how she treats animals, how her health will be affected, and how to ensure that she gets proper nutrition (discussed in chapter 4). Choose recipes together and have everyone in the family take turns cooking. Help her with school issues such as dissection. Let her know what she could eat while at fast food restaurants. Help her learn to handle peer pressure, which will be discussed fully in chapter 5. Help her find other vegan teens to talk to. There's a forum where she can chat with other vegan teens at www.vegfamily.com/forums.

What to do if your teen decides not to go vegan. You may be very disappointed if your teen decides not to go vegan, but don't be. If you live as an example, he could very well go vegan later in life. Just give him time, space, and understanding. Don't judge him or make him feel bad when he eats animal products. Keep the lines of communication open, and be sure he is aware of how animals are treated. Introduce him to vegan personal care products and see if he'll switch. Do what you can and leave the rest in his hands. Because of your influence, even if your teen does eat meat and dairy products he probably eats less of them than do other kids his age. And remember, it could be worse... eating meat or dairy products is not as bad as smoking, taking drugs, or drinking alcohol.

Should you stop buying non-vegan foods for your teen? You have to work this out between you and your teen. Some families set guidelines or rules, for example: "If you want meat and dairy you'll have to buy it and cook it yourself," or "I'll buy your food but you have to cook it yourself," or "In this house we eat vegan but what you do when you're at school or out with friends is your choice." Decide what will work best in your family.

Answering the Hard Questions

Even if your child seems willing to go vegan, there may come a time when she questions why she has to be a vegan. She may wish to try non-vegan foods because she's curious. Or maybe she'll want to know why her grandparents eat meat if it's wrong for *her* to eat meat. How will you answer her questions?

The key to handling these situations and answering the hard questions is preparation. Know in advance what you'll say and what you're willing to let your children do. If an unexpected situation crops up, handle it the best way you can. The following are some questions your child may ask you and some ideas for how to answer them.

"Mom, why does grandma eat meat?" Kids who have been told how bad meat is can become confused when they see it being consumed by people that they love. They want to know why grandma is being "bad." This is a good opportunity to teach your children tolerance. We teach our kids not to judge people of other races, religions, or creeds, and we need to extend that teaching to lifestyle choices as well. First, be sure she understands that just because others make different choices than we do doesn't mean they are "bad" people. Second, explain that when someone has been doing something for a long time, it's difficult to change. Be sure that you're being respectful in front of non-vegans so your child can see tolerance in action.

> **Real Stories from Real Parents:**
> *My daughter gets very distressed when she sees my mom and dad eating meat. I've told her that sometimes older people are set in their ways and that not everyone thinks the way we do. I told her we could feel sorry for them, but not to judge them. I do wish my parents wouldn't eat meat in front of her though.* – Melissa

When your child wants something non-vegan. Sometimes the sight of something non-vegan is too much for some kids. They want that cupcake with the thick frosting and colorful sprinkles on it. They know they shouldn't eat it, but they want it badly. First, validate his feelings and show him that you understand why he would want something like that. "That cupcake sure looks good, doesn't it?" Then inform him why he shouldn't eat it: "I think it has cow's milk in it, dear, so it's not vegan. Sorry." If that does it, great. If he still wants it, offer him a vegan alternative, even if it means waiting a little to get it. "Hey, why don't we make cupcakes when we get home?"

Real Stories from Real Parents:
When my daughter sees something she wants and it isn't vegan I say, "That's not vegan, sweetie." If she resists, I'll say, "I know it looks good, doesn't it? But it has dairy in it." That usually does the trick. – Melanie

---

"Dad, what happens to animals who are made into food?" How you answer this question depends entirely on your child's age and ability to handle graphic details. I believe in being truthful with children of all ages; it's just a matter of how many of the details to divulge. Following are some ideas, but obviously you know your child best, so use your own judgment regarding what to say.

For children between four and eight, you could say, "Animals are raised in cages and they are not treated very well. They're very unhappy. One day someone comes and takes them away and sells them in a grocery store to people who eat meat. The animals are not happy about this at all and wish people would stop eating them. That's why we're vegans, to help the animals."

For children between the ages of eight and 12, you could say, "Animals are raised in cages and they are not treated well at all. They'd like to be out of their cages running free and interacting with their friends, but they can't. The poor animals often get diseases and injuries and no one really helps them much. It's a very distressing life for an animal. Eventually, the animal is killed and sent to a grocery store, where people will buy it and eat it. It's all very sad."

Kids older than 12 can probably stand to hear more of the details, or you may want to give them books, literature, or let them watch videos about how animals are raised and slaughtered. Always view these items before letting your kids see them. It can be very upsetting to see what really happens to animals when you're not prepared for it.

"Why do some parents make their kids eat meat?" Once a child understands that a vegan diet is healthy, and is good for the animals, and that eating meat and dairy products are unhealthy and cruel, he may become distressed to see his friends eating animal products. He may think they are being forced by their parents to do so. You can say, "Not everyone knows that eating meat is unhealthy and cruel. They think they're doing the right thing by giving their kids meat. I hope that in time they'll realize they were misinformed and stop giving their kids meat. Until then, just continue to be a good example for them and don't judge them."

"Do I have to be vegan all the time?" Some kids think that if they've been "good" they can cheat a little. It's important to instill in them the idea that what they're doing is not temporary, and isn't subject to rewards. You could say, "Well, honey, if you ate that scoop of ice cream you'd be hurting an animal. I know it may not seem that way, but when you eat something made from an animal it hurts them. Even if you just do it one time, it still hurts them."

"Why do I have to be a vegan?" If the child who asks this is very young, try explaining how poorly animals are treated. You can try to put them in the place of the animal and give them a sense of how it might feel to end up as someone's dinner.

If your child is older, tell her of the many wonderful benefits of being a vegan, such as being kind to animals, living with a clear conscience, being healthy, and helping the environment.

If your child is a teen, you may not be as successful in answering this question to his satisfaction. Tell him how proud you are of him for being a vegan. Remind him of the positive impact he is having on the planet. Let him know how special he is for being a vegan and living cruelty-free. At the very least, ask your teen to be respectful by eating vegan in your home, and not to flaunt it when he eats non-vegan outside the home.

"If eating meat is so bad, how come we ate it before?" Some children become disconcerted when they realize what they were eating before going vegan. Mention that you only recently learned how animals suffer and how unhealthy it is to eat animal products. Explain that when a person discovers he's been doing something wrong, the only thing he can do is make changes and go on from there.

"How come Susie can eat that, but I can't?" Young children who don't fully comprehend why they're vegans may be confused when children around them are receiving something that they themselves are not allowed to have. For example, at a birthday party, the children might receive bags of non-vegan candy. When the host goes to give your child one, you politely decline on behalf of your child. Your child turns to you and says, "How come I can't have that? Susie got one." You could say, "That candy has animal products in it, honey. We don't eat that kind of candy. Susie is allowed to eat that kind of candy because she's not a vegan." If you want, you can also add, "We'll get some vegan candy on the way home from the party, OK?" Or "Look, I brought some of your favorite chocolate chip cookies to eat instead of candy."

What About Mixed Marriages?
What happens when one parent is vegan and the other one isn't? Will the children be raised vegan or not? If you are a

vegan but your spouse or partner is not, and you have or are planning to have children, then you are in what I call a mixed marriage. Families in this situation have some challenges to overcome and some difficult decisions to make. The good news is that it is entirely possible to raise your children vegan even if your partner is not a vegan. But it's not easy.

I believe there are two prerequisites for successfully raising vegan children in a mixed marriage. First, your partner must agree that it is healthy for a child to be a vegan. Second, your partner must agree to be an active participant in raising the children vegan. If you don't have those two commitments from your non-vegan partner, then it's unlikely that your children will be raised totally vegan. If your partner does not believe it's healthy for children to be vegan, he or she will subconsciously – or outright – sabotage your efforts to raise the children vegan. Similarly, if your spouse has not agreed to raise the children vegan, and is not willing to participate in ensuring that the children are raised vegan, then you two will constantly be at odds about what to feed the kids. That's a sure way to create conflict in a marriage or partnership.

Assuming that your partner has agreed to raise the children vegan, here are some guidelines for a successful outcome.

Set ground rules. The families I interviewed who are in mixed marriages say that it's important that everyone is clear about how food will be treated in the home. Conflict will arise if the rules are unclear or if one person expects a certain behavior from the other and doesn't get it. Make sure that whatever rules you come up with are agreed upon by both partners and are completely understood. The following are examples of rules that other families have adopted.

- Only vegan meals are served in the home.
- Only vegan groceries are allowed in the home.

- The non-vegan spouse may eat meat at a restaurant or away from home only.
- The non-vegan spouse will not eat meat in front of the children.
- Certain sections of the refrigerator and freezer may contain meat, but it is limited to those sections only, and is off limits to the children.
- The non-vegan spouse may eat meat in the home but only if he cooks it himself.
- At parties or family events, the non-vegan spouse should try to refrain from eating meat and dairy products in front of the children, if at all possible.

Make eating vegan fun for everyone. If you've decided that only vegan meals will be served in your home, try to find recipes that will appeal to everyone, including the non-vegan parent. There are lots of dishes that non-vegans will readily eat even if there is no meat or dairy in them. For example, spaghetti with marinara sauce, stir-fried vegetables, lasagna, pizza, or falafel sandwiches. Let your non-vegan partner select some vegan recipes he or she likes and serve them often. If cooking is not your forte, you can now find an abundance of convenient, frozen vegan meals at health food stores. They are easy to make and are definite crowd pleasers. For a list of these products, see www.vegfamily.com/product-reviews/index.htm.

Be respectful. Don't disparage or berate your spouse in front of your children. If she eats meat at the table and you cluck in disapproval, your children will feel uncomfortable and confused. Similarly, teach your children that not everyone is a vegan, and to be respectful and tolerant of everyone's lifestyle.

Educate your partner. Be sure your non-vegan partner knows what is vegan and what isn't, including hidden animal ingredients. Inevitably there will be times when your partner is alone with the kids at an event where non-vegan foods are being served. If he doesn't like to read labels or ask questions, or doesn't know what questions to ask, your children may end up accidentally eating something non-vegan. Plan ahead, be prepared, send vegan foods along with your family, and remind your children to ask whether something is vegan before they eat it.

> **Real Stories from Real Parents:**
> *One day my husband took our daughter to a friend's house to watch the Superbowl. I met them there an hour or so later and found her munching on a cracker. When I asked him if he'd checked the label, he said that crackers are just flour and water. I was pretty annoyed with him. I found the box they were from and there were three varieties. One was vegan, but the other two had dairy in them. So I made sure she ate the vegan ones and when we got home we talked about it. I was frustrated, not only because of the ethics, but because there could have been egg in it! She could have been sick and vomiting and miserable because he didn't bother to read the label. He's been more careful since, but I do have to be the one to monitor things more closely.*
>
> *I really wish he would take a more active role when it comes to things like that. I definitely wish he were a vegan so we could share the commitment and the difficulties, like planning ahead and getting stressed about parties and restaurants!* – Ellen

Present a united front. When you're at an event with family, friends, or co-workers, it's important that your non-vegan spouse doesn't abandon you to fend off comments and/or criticisms of adversarial people. Also, if some member of the family is constantly pressuring you to feed your children meat or dairy products, be sure that both you and your spouse – not just the partner who is the vegan – defend the decision to raise vegan children. If the non-vegan parent says nothing, it will be much harder on the vegan parent. This is especially true if you meet resistance from your partner's family because you may not feel as comfortable asserting yourself.

Don't be too hard on yourself or the kids. If your kids do eat something they shouldn't, or if they occasionally try something their non-vegan parent is eating, don't get angry. Often it's just a one-time experiment. Sometimes children find that the non-vegan food makes them sick or doesn't taste very good. These experiences may actually serve to reinforce their vegan lifestyle. So instead of getting upset just guide them gently back to veganism, remind them why you're vegan, and continue to be proud of their accomplishments.

If the "unthinkable" happens and your kids decide to give up being vegan to eat meat and dairy products, don't be too hard on yourself. Your kids will probably be eating better than most kids their age because of your vegan influence. And who knows, in the future, they may go vegan again.

When things fall apart. Two couples whom I interviewed each had one partner transition to being a vegan while their spouse did not, and they were unable to transition their children to veganism. This was because the partner ate meat in front of the children and bought the children whatever they wanted when they were outside of the home. Arguments about how the kids would eat were straining these marriages to the breaking point. You have to ask yourself which is more important: that your kids be vegan or that there is harmony in the home. The fact is, legally, your partner has just as much input as to what the kids eat as you do. If you end up getting divorced because you can't see eye to eye on this issue, then your kids will eat vegan with you and eat non-vegan when they're with your ex-spouse anyway. Is that really what you want to happen?

If you find yourself arguing constantly about this issue, sit down with your partner and make a diligent effort to learn about her fears, issues, or doubts concerning raising vegan children. Maybe you can clarify something also, maybe not. Maybe you'll decide that your kids eat vegan at home but they can have whatever they want outside the home. You'll have to compromise and so will your partner.

Respect the rules. If you've agreed that your kids can eat what they want outside the home, don't make nasty comments when they eat meat in a restaurant. Similarly, your partner should not make comments at the dinner table like, "Eww, tofu again? I'd rather have chicken." Be respectful of the rules you've agreed upon. You won't have totally vegan children, but you will have respect, harmony, a better marriage, and healthier kids than most.

Don't forget, you can still practice other aspects of veganism, such as compassion towards animals, using non-animal products in the home, recycling, and buying from vegan-owned companies. You will still make a tremendous difference!

Real Stories from Real Parents:
I understand and respect my wife for having the will power to live a vegan lifestyle. I find it inspiring at times. I just don't seem to have the commitment that she does. I love to eat all kinds of food, vegan and non-vegan alike. I know that a vegan lifestyle is healthier and better for the earth as well. I haven't reached that level - yet.

When it comes to Kaya (our daughter), it seems to me that if she does not know about eating meat or dairy products, then she won't miss them. So raising her vegan from the start seems perfectly natural to me. That being said, if Ellen wasn't vegan I don't think that I would raise Kaya vegan. I would certainly be eating a lot more meat and dairy products. – Doug

---

Educating Family and Friends

If you're lucky, your friends and family will embrace the fact that you've gone vegan and will think it's wonderful that your child is going to be a vegan too. But what if you tell them you're going vegan and you receive a less than enthusiastic response? What if they question whether it's healthy to raise vegan children (i.e., "Well it's fine for you, but is that really fair to impose your beliefs on your kids? Where will they get their protein?") What if they won't abide by your decision and decide to sneak your child bits of meat and dairy products when you're not around? What if they are so concerned that you're harming your child that they decide to report you to Child Protective Services?

When you announce to people that you and your children are going vegan you should be prepared to deal with their ignorance, fear, and concern. If you don't address it and give it the attention it deserves, you could have a serious problem on your hands in the form of a knock at your door one day from a social worker. Here are tips and guidelines for helping your friends and family deal with the new situation.

Explaining veganism to your family. Some people tell their families that they're going vegan and no one bats an eyelash. Other people tell their families about their change in lifestyle and are immediately bombarded with questions, doubt, fear, and alarm. You'll have an easier time getting your family to accept your decision if you're prepared, well-read on the subject, and can answer all their questions. After you've been vegan for a while, they'll see that you're not dying a slow death.

Your friends and family members care about you and your child, and will likely express their concerns. Be sure you can answer questions about where your kids will get their protein, calcium, and iron (chapter 4), how you will help your children deal with being "different" in school (chapter 5), and how they are going to deal with other kids' birthday parties and similar social situations (chapter 6).

Read some books about being vegan. Have some statistics handy for the logical people in your family. Show them that you've done your homework so that it will be easier for your family to trust your decision. It will also show them that you're taking the subject seriously, which could be important later if they decide to legally challenge your right to raise vegan children.

Get ready to answer a lot of questions. Here are some you're likely to be asked and some suggestions for how to answer them:

"Where will she get her protein?" "All foods contain protein. There are plenty of foods in the vegan diet that are high in protein, like tofu, beans, nuts, and legumes. As long as she is getting enough calories each day, and is eating a varied diet, I'm confident she'll get enough protein."

"Don't you have to combine proteins to form complete amino acid chains?" "No, that's old information. New studies show that combining proteins is unnecessary. The body holds on to the amino acids it's accumulated throughout the day and pairs them to form complete proteins."

"Where will he get calcium?" "Milk and dairy products aren't the only foods that contain calcium, nor are they the most absorbable sources of calcium. He'll get calcium from green leafy vegetables, broccoli, nuts, soymilk, tofu, and fortified juices. If I'm really concerned, he'll get a supplement. But more importantly, he won't be eating foods that leach calcium out of the body."

"They'll make fun of your kids in school." "Kids will find a way to make fun of any person they want, whether they tease him for being too short or too round, wearing glasses, being the teacher's pet, being vegan, etc. I'll teach my child how to protect himself from schoolyard bullies."

"You're depriving your child of so much." "Yes, I'm depriving her of heart disease, cancer, high blood pressure, strokes, diabetes, and obesity."

"But what if she wants to eat meat? Will you stop her?" "When she's old enough to make her own decisions, she can do what she wants. Until then, I will decide what's best for her, like any parent does."

"No child can be healthy without eating meat or dairy products." "If that were true, then how could hundreds of thousands of children who are being raised vegan in this world still be alive and healthier than kids who eat meat? I'm afraid the evidence just doesn't agree with you."

"How's he going to feel if he's the only one not eating birthday cake at a party?" "He'll be eating birthday cake at parties; it will just be a cake I've made for him. How do diabetic children cope with not being able to eat cake at parties? What do kosher children eat at a non-kosher party?"

"But all his friends will be eating meat. He'll want to do it too." "And if all his friends started smoking cigarettes, am I supposed to sit back and watch it happen without intervening? As he grows up and matures he'll understand why we don't eat animals, and he'll most likely agree with the reasoning behind it."

"Do you have to be so strict?" "What you see as being strict, I see as being refreshingly liberated. My child will go to bed each night with a clear conscience and a healthy body."

However you decide to answer their questions, I urge you not to get into heated debates or arguments. You don't have to prove anything to anyone. If someone tries to draw you into a debate you can say, "That's your opinion. I do not agree," or "I'm not interested in debating this issue with you. I'm very comfortable with my decision." One thing that often works in getting family off your back is to say, "I'd be happy to discuss the merits of raising vegan children with you *after* you've done some research and educated yourself on the matter. Until then, discussing the situation with you really wouldn't be that useful to me."

My final piece of advice when it comes to explaining veganism to your family is simply to live by example. When they see that your family is getting healthier and healthier, it will be hard for them to argue their case, and they may begin asking *you* for advice! The proof is in the tofu pudding, so to speak. Be a healthy, vegan family and your relatives will see a healthy, vegan family.

Helping your family take care of your vegan child. If your family helps you care for your child, you've got to be sure they know what they're doing. You don't want to pick up your child one day and discover that your mother gave her tuna fish, but conscientiously took out the eggs and mayonnaise. Well-intentioned people make honest mistakes all the time. Here are some things to watch out for.

First, make sure that whoever is spending time alone with your child knows exactly what foods your child can and cannot eat. If you need to, make a list and tape it to their refrigerator. Warn them about hidden ingredients and show them what to look for on labels.

Second, make it easy on them. My parents take care of my daughter often, but they never know what to feed her. I bring over some foods that I know she'll eat and put them in the refrigerator, freezer, and pantry so that my parents don't have to think about it. They know they can just grab something from her stash and it's been pre-approved. Examples of items I bring over are: frozen waffles, juice, energy bars, peanut butter, jelly, bread, fake chicken nuggets, fresh fruit, pudding, crackers, soup, and occasionally, a frozen pizza.

Third, if your relatives are going to take your child out to eat and you're not going to be there, be sure they know how to order for your child in a restaurant. Restaurants are full of foods with hidden animal ingredients. In chapter 4 we'll cover tips for dining out.

> **Real Stories from Real Parents:**
> *My parents don't feel comfortable asking lots of questions in restaurants, so I find out where they're taking my daughter and tell them what to order for her. If they're ever out and they're not sure, I tell them to look for baked potatoes (dry), french fries, sourdough toast with jelly only, a peanut butter and jelly sandwich, steamed veggies, steamed rice, or a fruit plate. Those are the items that nearly all restaurants can come up with in a pinch.* – Daria

When family doesn't agree with your decision to raise vegan children. There may be some members of your family who simply cannot see how raising a child vegan is a good thing. If they truly want to understand your reasoning, give them some books on the subject. If they aren't interested in learning what you know, then there's no point in arguing with them. Whatever you do, don't get defensive. If they have a problem with how you raise your kids, it's their problem, not yours.

When family won't abide by your decision. What if your relatives think they're doing your child a favor by slipping him bits of meat and cheese when you're not looking? You've got to stop that behavior immediately. Treat it the same way as if they were giving your child a sip of alcohol or a drag on a cigarette. Leave the environment; take your child away from their influence until you are sure your family can be trusted to support the lifestyle you've chosen for your child. Consistency is very important to children. If you need to interact with your family, be sure that either you or your partner is always watching the children to make sure that they aren't fed animal products.

When family threatens you with legal action. It's a sad state of affairs when your own family threatens to call Child Protective Services (CPS) on you simply for raising a child without meat and dairy products. I'm sorry I even have to include this information, but I do. I've heard of, read, and/or been involved in cases where a well-meaning grandparent or in-law has called CPS and reported that their grandchildren were not getting appropriate nutrition because they were being raised vegan. Do you know what happens after that call is made? It's not pretty. CPS comes to your door, sits you down, and interrogates you about what you feed your child. Suddenly the burden of proof is on you. If you don't convince these people that your child is healthy, they have the authority to remove your child from your home pending an investigation. Sometimes the child is put in foster care while the case is being documented, and I can assure you the foster parents won't be feeding your child a vegan diet.

If anyone in your family makes a threat like this, take it seriously. Do whatever you can to make them understand that your child is healthy. One of the best things you can do to avoid legal trouble is to have your child seen by a doctor periodically so there is documented evidence that your child was healthy and well at the time of the exam. Also, you must be certain that you are feeding your child a proper vegan diet. Study chapter 4 on nutrition and occasionally ask yourself if you're sure your child is getting all he needs from this diet. It's a shame that vegans have to prove their diet is healthy when a diet of meat and dairy products does more harm than a well-balanced diet of fruits, vegetables, nuts, grains, and legumes. No one ever seems to call Child Protective Services on families for serving their children meat and dairy products or taking them to McDonald's four times a week!

If worse comes to worst and your child is removed from your home pending an investigation, contact the

Physicians Committee for Responsible Medicine at www.pcrm.org, get a good family lawyer, contact vegan organizations such as PETA and EarthSave International, and if need be, get the vegan community to support you by writing to influential members of the vegan press and asking them to cover your story.

Avoidance is key. Don't let this happen to you. I hope none of you will ever have to go through something like this.

Real Stories from Real Parents:
I have only a few relatives who don't understand my and my husband's choice to raise our children vegan. They make comments based on their ignorance of the health aspects of a vegan diet, like "Your son is so small because he doesn't eat meat!" Sometimes they have given our children snacks that had milk in them, which made them sick. We have to be diligent in taking those items away from our kids and explaining to our relatives that it's not OK to give our kids non-vegan snacks. Over time the situation has improved, and now they don't make as many snide comments. As a bonus, because my children are healthy, several of my relatives have cut back on meat and given up dairy completely. Not bad for a couple of kids. –Tabitha

---

Explaining veganism to your friends. Explaining your new lifestyle to friends won't be nearly as challenging as explaining it to family. Your friends are more likely to embrace the new you, want to know what you're eating, and want to know how to feed your kids when they come over for a play date.

As with family, make it easy on your friends by giving them a list of what your child can and cannot eat. And always offer to send a vegan snack with your child if she's going to a friend's house, at least initially. You'll probably find that they are very supportive of your new lifestyle.

Be sure not to get preachy or proselytize your diet, because that will only put your friends on the defensive. Don't be disapproving of their diets. If you really want your friends to move towards veganism, be an example and let your child's health serve as a model of the positive benefits of raising vegan children. Be there to answer their questions; your example will be the best influence.

If any of your friends will not accept that you're raising your child vegan, it may be time to let those friends go. After all, you don't want to find out that your friend is giving your child string cheese when you're not around. People who cannot accept you the way you are and respect your parenting decisions are not your friends.

Chapter 3

HEALTH

There are a lot of questions to answer when it comes to raising healthy children on a vegan diet. Are vegans really healthier than meat eaters? What are the tangible benefits of a vegan diet? How do doctors react when they learn that your children are being raised vegan, how can you handle any negative reactions, and is it possible to find an understanding doctor to care for your children? Do vegan children need vitamins or will they get all the nutrients they need from diet alone? Are all vaccines vegan? What risks does your child face if he is not vaccinated? What about drugs and medicines; are those vegan? Is there a way to keep your kids healthy without resorting to non-vegan medicines?

By the end of this chapter, you will have answers to these questions, and you will be confident that raising vegan children is the best way to give them a healthy start in life.

Health Benefits of Being Vegan
In my opinion, the health benefits of being vegan are extraordinary. I have first-hand knowledge of how going vegan can significantly improve one's health. Before going vegan my total cholesterol count was 293 and my HDL (the "good" cholesterol) was 21. Within three months of going vegan my total cholesterol dropped to 253 and my HDL more soared to 71. My triglycerides plummeted from 390 to

144. Ninety percent of my allergy symptoms disappeared. My skin became smooth (even around my elbows!), and my nails became stronger than they'd ever been before. Before going vegan I would often take two antacids per day; afterwards, I had to donate my entire bottle to other members of my family. Today, there are no antacids in my medicine cabinet because I don't ever need them. I stopped getting diarrhea and food poisoning. My frequent headaches became infrequent headaches. The aches and pains in my joints disappeared, and my carpal tunnel syndrome melted away. During this three month period I also lost approximately 20 pounds, easily, and without decreasing my caloric intake. My energy increased. And though I can't document this, I believe my mental clarity improved as well. No one had to convince me that going vegan was good for my health. I woke up every morning feeling like a new person.

But don't just take my word for it; doctors and scientists all over the world have researched the health benefits of being vegan. Following are some of the benefits a vegan diet will afford you and your children.

Prevent heart disease. Heart disease is the leading cause of death in America. Everyone knows that high cholesterol leads to atherosclerosis – hardening of the arteries – which can cause a heart attack. Cholesterol is found only in animal products, so vegans are getting zero cholesterol from their diets. That's right, *zero* cholesterol! A diet high in saturated fat can contribute to heart disease, as well. Most saturated fat comes from animal products, so you won't be getting that either. You may also know that fiber helps prevent heart disease because it lowers your cholesterol. How lucky for you that the vegan diet is very high in fiber! In fact, the foods highest in fiber are fruits, vegetables, and legumes, which are staples in the vegan diet. Alas, animal products contain no fiber at all. So your diet is already protecting you from the main causes of heart disease. Now all you have to do is exercise, say no to smoking and alcohol, decrease your stress, be sure you're breathing clean air, and drink pure water. If you already suffer from heart disease, being vegan will help you reverse the effects of atherosclerosis.

Prevent cancer. According to the Physicians Committee for Responsible Medicine (www.pcrm.org), cancer rates for vegetarians are, on average, 25 to 50 percent below population averages. Many cancers, such as colon, prostate, and breast cancer, are highly associated with meat and dairy consumption. Including fruits and vegetables in the daily diet will decrease your risk for cancers of the lung, breast, colon, bladder, stomach, mouth, larynx, esophagus, pancreas, cervix, and prostate. Getting abundant fiber and vitamins reduces the risk of cancer. Also, vegans have higher levels of specialized white blood cells, called natural killer cells, that attack cancer cells. As you can see, being vegan can be a great way to prevent cancer.

Avoid other health problems. There are several other degenerative diseases, conditions, and ailments which can be prevented or significantly improved by being vegan. Because vegan diets are high in vitamins, minerals, antioxidants, and fiber, are low in saturated fat, and are devoid of animal protein and cholesterol, you *may* never see problems like diabetes, gallstones, kidney stones, arthritis, iron deficiency anemia, osteoporosis, high blood pressure, asthma, and some food allergies. If you do already suffer from any of these ailments, it will probably improve when you go vegan. Further, young children will probably suffer less from colic and chronic ear infections on a vegan diet.

Boost your immune system. Vegan diets are rich in foods that help boost the immune system. Fruits and vegetables contain vitamins, minerals, and antioxidants. These foods will help you fight off illness and recover from illness faster. Avoiding dairy means less mucous, and avoiding meat means less carcinogens. It all adds up to a superior immune system.

Evade foodborne illnesses. Most foodborne illness comes from eating meat and dairy products. Being vegan will help you avoid salmonella, E. coli, trichinosis, and campylobacter to name a few. Think about the last time you got sick because you ate a bad peach. Now think of the times you've been up all night vomiting from eating greasy, undercooked meat or spoiled potato salad. When people get food poisoning, you rarely hear them asking, "What was in that apple cobbler we ate last night?" Instead, you'll hear, "It must have been the turkey."

Say goodbye to antibiotics and hormones. Food animals are often injected with antibiotics, hormones, and steroids, which go right into your child when he eats meat and dairy products. By raising your child vegan, you're protecting him from receiving daily doses of these chemicals.

Elude pesticides and herbicides. Toxic residue accumulates in the tissue of animals who eat grains that were sprayed with herbicides and pesticides. It's much easier to wash pesticide residue off an apple (or peel it) than to get it out of a steak. Buy organic whenever possible!

Dodge toxins. Dioxin is one of the most dangerous toxins a person can ingest, and it is suspected of causing an inordinate amount of human cancers. And where is dioxin found? It's in meat, dairy, and fish products. Other toxins like DDT, dieldrin, heptachlor, and PCBs, also pollute meat and dairy products. And sadly, the breast milk of women who eat meat and dairy products contains alarmingly high amounts of pesticide residues which are passed directly on to their babies.

Live longer. *Vegetarian Diets for Children: Right from the Start*, published by the PCRM, states that, "Vegetarian children grow up to be slimmer, healthier, and live longer than their meat-eating friends." Not only will you and your children live longer, you will all probably suffer less from the debilitating effects of aging.

Selecting a Health Care Professional
It's possible that when you take your child to the pediatrician, he will cast doubt and suspicion on the merits of a vegan diet, if you choose to mention it to him in the first place. The doctor may even encourage you to feed your child dairy products and a "little fish so she can get some protein." But let me give you a word of warning. Most doctors have studied very little nutrition. There's an excellent chance that you know more about nutrition than the doctor. Just because he's standing there in his own office wearing a stethoscope and a white coat doesn't mean he's a nutrition expert. Far from it; most doctors get less than five hours of nutrition education during their time in medical school. Do you ever ask your doctor for advice about the rattling sound under the hood of your car? No! You ask a professional in that field; a mechanic. For expert advice on diet and nutrition, see a veg-friendly dietician, not a doctor.

If your doctor launches into a lecture about why being vegan isn't healthy, you can either counter all of his arguments with facts and statistics, or simply say, "I see we have a difference of opinion. The research I've done suggests otherwise."

If you happen to have a doctor who understands the health benefits of a vegan diet, consider yourself lucky. If you don't see this kind of doctor, it might be time to find a qualified health care professional who will applaud you for raising vegan children. Here's how to go about finding such a person.

Get referrals from your vegan friends. If you've got vegan or vegetarian friends, ask them who their doctor is and whether the doctor is accepting of their diet. Avoid doctors who berate, lecture, or browbeat your friends for being vegetarian.

Hang out in the health food store. Health food stores are great resources for information. Many people who work in health food stores are vegans themselves. Strike up a conversation with one of the grocery clerks and, if you find out they are vegan, tell them you're looking for a vegan-friendly doctor in the area and see if they have a recommendation for you.

If you see vegan parents shopping with their kids, ask them for referrals too. How can you tell they're vegan? Just glance at their carts to see if there are any meat or dairy products inside.

You may even see people carrying canvas bags or wearing shirts from vegan or animal rights organizations. Those are good clues that they might be vegan.

Ask around online. It's a long shot, but if you go online and visit some vegan message boards, you might be able to find someone living in your area who can give you a good recommendation.

Look outside conventional medicine. You don't have to take your child to a standard or conventional pediatrician. You can see a homeopathic physician, chiropractor, naturopath, or even an acupuncturist. Traditional doctors aren't the only ones who can treat people. Always make sure that the health care professional you choose is qualified. Get referrals from their patients or from your friends.

Educate your pediatrician. If your insurance won't cover seeing someone else and you can't afford to pay out-of-pocket, try educating your current pediatrician on the benefits of a vegan diet. Be tactful in your approach. You can offer to bring literature that points out the merits of a vegan diet. Refer to the ADA paper, which states, "appropriately planned vegetarian diets are healthful, are nutritionally adequate, and provide health benefits in the prevention and treatment of certain diseases." The paper goes further and affirms, "appropriately planned vegan and lacto-ovo-vegetarian diets satisfy nutrient needs of infants, children, and adolescents and promote normal growth." Let her know that you've done your research and that you're confident in your ability to raise a healthy vegan child. Give her a list of books by registered vegan dieticians that discuss the nutritional benefits of raising vegan children (see www.vegfamily.com/book-reviews/index.htm for a list). You can always use this line, "After all doctor, my child eats more fruits and vegetables in one day than most kids eat in a week. Wouldn't you say that's healthy?" I doubt most doctors would argue with that. Keep your tone light and friendly, and be confident as well.

Whatever happens, don't let any health care professional browbeat you or harass you about raising your children vegan. In 1997, when I first went vegan, I had a conversation with a woman who had raised her son vegan in the 1970's. One day she took her son to the doctor and mentioned in passing that she didn't feed her son cow's milk or other dairy products. When she revealed that she was raising him vegan, the doctor reported her to social services. They came to her house and ransacked her refrigerator. Finding no meat or dairy products, they told her that if she didn't start feeding her son milk, he would be taken away from her and she would be charged with neglect or abuse. She was so frightened that she started buying milk and meat and keeping them in her refrigerator so that when social services came back it would "look" like she was feeding him these things, even though she was not. That was decades ago, and I'd like to think that in this day and age something like that wouldn't happen, that doctors don't threaten to call social services on vegan parents, but I'd be wrong. I've been contacted by half a dozen parents who were facing problems with Social Services simply because they were raising their children vegan. If you suspect your doctor is the type who might view veganism as child abuse, I strongly urge to you to find someone who will support your choices.

> **Real Stories from Real Parents:**
> *When my daughter was starting table foods, I asked my pediatrician about her being vegetarian. He told me that we couldn't do that since she needed the fat from meat to have healthy brain growth. So much for trusting your doctor to know what's best for your child! Today she and my son are both happy, healthy, vegan children. I know I am doing the best for them now that we are vegans. I have not mentioned a word to my pediatrician, and he is none the wiser.* – Tabitha

Are Vitamins Necessary?

Parents often worry that their kids aren't getting enough vitamins and nutrients from the foods they eat. This may be a valid concern if you are new to veganism, haven't yet incorporated whole foods into the diet, have picky kids who won't try new things, or if you cook all the nutrients out of your foods before serving them. If you fall into one of these categories, here's what you need to know about supplementing with vitamins.

New to veganism. People new to veganism may be unaware that there are a few vitamins and nutrients that are slightly more difficult to obtain on a vegan diet than on an omnivorous one. B_{12} and fatty acids are two nutrients that vegans must consciously include in their diets. We'll discuss all the important nutrients and the best sources of them in the next chapter. Until you've got a reliable source of these nutrients in your child's diet, you may want to supplement with a vitamin.

New to whole foods. I'll never forget a conversation I had over dinner with Ann Gentry and her husband, Robert Jacobs, about the importance of incorporating whole foods into the diet. Ann is the founder of *Real Food Daily*, a gourmet, organic, vegan restaurant located in Los Angeles. I told her I had recently gone vegan and eliminated meat and dairy products from my diet. She asked if I had incorporated whole foods into my diet to make up for the loss of meat and dairy, or if I continued to eat white flour, canned vegetables, canned fruit, and junk food. I admitted to the latter. She and her husband spent the rest of dinner educating me on the importance of getting whole and organic foods into my diet.

If you think that all you have to do for your kids is stop giving them meat and dairy, you've only half the story. You also need to stop giving them foods devoid of nutrition, and start giving them foods full of health and whole vitamins. Bread and pasta made with white flour have had many nutrients stripped out of them and then substituted artificially. Sure, it's vegan, but it's not healthy. Switch to using whole grains like whole wheat, barley, quinoa, and millet, instead of white flour.

Beware of non-nutritive juice. The juice you are giving your child should be pure 100% fruit, not made from high fructose corn syrup. Otherwise you're just filling her belly with empty calories and refined sugars. If she wants to drink juice, make it yourself from real fruit. For some great smoothie recipes, see www.vegfamily.com/vegan-pregnancy/fruit-smoothies.htm.

The canning process also destroys enzymes and strips vital nutrients from fruits, vegetables, and legumes. When at all possible, give your children whole fruit, whole vegetables, and un-canned legumes.

Nuts and seeds retain their nutrients as long as they are raw and unroasted. I know they are a lot blander that way, but you don't have to eat them by the handfuls. Use raw nuts to make butters or creams. Or throw some raw almonds or cashews into a salad.

Until your kids are eating whole grain, nutritious foods, you may want to give them a vitamin supplement.

Picky eaters. If your child is new to veganism, she may not be too enamored with the new foods coming out of your kitchen. Tofu scramble is going to be less appealing than scrambled eggs, initially. She may latch on to a few favorites and avoid trying new things. Until she's eating a varied and balanced diet, you may want to supplement with vitamins. Rest assured that in time she'll embrace the new foods. For more information on handling picky eaters, refer to chapter 4.

Cooking the nutrients out of your food. You probably already know that when you boil vegetables a lot of the nutrients are lost. The same is true, but to a lesser extent, when you stir-fry, deep-fry, or sauté your vegetables. When at all possible, serve fruits and vegetables in their raw state so that their vital nutrients go directly into the body.

When you do cook vegetables, bake or steam them so they'll retain more of their nutrients. Until you're doing this regularly, you may want to offer your kids a multi-vitamin supplement.

The bottom line on vitamins. It's entirely possible for your child to get all the vitamins and minerals he needs on a vegan diet, but if you are at all uncertain that your child is getting them, then there's nothing wrong with supplementing with a vegan vitamin. It's better to be safe than sorry. Vitamin deficiencies, especially in children under three, can cause severe health problems. You don't want to risk that. For a list of companies that offer vegan vitamins for kids (and adults) see, www.vegfamily.com/product-reviews/index.htm.

What's the Deal With Vaccines?
You might be wondering what vaccines have to do with veganism. I wondered that myself back in 1998 when my husband told me that he wanted to discuss whether to vaccinate our future children. We had both been fully vaccinated as children, so I couldn't imagine what issue he might have. He pointed me to some information, Web sites, and books that called into question the efficacy of vaccinating while pointing out the dangers associated with

vaccinating. He gave me a list of vaccine ingredients that he'd found on the Internet. Suffice it to say, many if not all vaccines contain animal products as well as ingredients considered harmful, like formaldehyde, mercury, and aluminum.

I had a very hard time with this issue. I grew up believing that vaccines prevent disease, but much of the literature and books I have since read concluded that there is no direct evidence that vaccines prevent disease. In fact, there was some question about vaccines *causing* disease and causing other ailments and degenerative disorders. I also learned that immunity wears off in time so, for example, if you vaccinate a child against chickenpox when he is three years old, it might wear off when he's 17. Getting chickenpox as a teenager or adult presents more danger than getting the illness as a young child. I didn't know what to do.

The more I read, the more I came to side with those people who are opposed to vaccinating. For me, what it came down to was this: If I inject my child with a vaccine, I know for sure that I am exposing her to a variety of toxins and animal ingredients, all for the sake of *possibly* preventing a disease she may *never* get. If I don't vaccinate her, she may not even get the disease, but if she does there's every reason to believe she will recover from it easily. My husband and I spent two years reading, researching, and discussing this very serious issue. I attended lectures from people on both sides of the controversy. In the end, we decided against vaccinating our daughter. It's a personal choice. I encourage you to do your own research so you're comfortable with your decision. For a list of helpful resources and books on this issue, see www.vegfamily.com/lists/vaccines.htm.

Vaccine ingredients. Vaccines are made with ingredients that would make anyone cringe. Can you imagine injecting the following ingredients directly into your child's veins? Ethylene glycol (antifreeze), phenol, formaldehyde, aluminum, thimerosal (a form of mercury), and neomycin and streptomycin (antibiotics).

Vaccines are also grown in and strained through animal or human tissue, like monkey kidney tissue, chicken embryo, embryonic guinea pig cells, calf serum, human diploid cells (the dissected organs of aborted human fetuses) as in the case of the rubella, hepatitis A, and chickenpox vaccines. Like any lab animal, those used in the production of vaccines are not treated well. And there is some discussion about the possibility that Mad Cow Disease may be transmissible through vaccines. Consider all this carefully when you make your decision.

What if your child gets sick? If you're concerned that your child will come down with measles, mumps, or chickenpox, read Dr. Robert Mendelsohn's book, *How to Raise a Healthy Child in Spite of Your Doctor,* in which he reassures and explains how to treat the diseases we currently vaccinate against. This book really set my mind at ease. I discovered that these illnesses are rarely complicated, and are unlikely to cause irreparable damage to the human body.

How will you get your child into school? Worried that your child won't be able to go to school without her shots? Don't be. You have the legal right to refuse to vaccinate your child. School officials who tell you that your child will not be allowed to enter school without being vaccinated are using intimidation tactics. Each state in the U.S. allows parents to exempt their child from receiving vaccines on the basis of personal, religious, and/or medical reasons. You must check your state's laws to find out what exemptions are allowed in your state. To do this, call or write your state representative and ask her for a copy of the immunization laws in your state. Making this information available is part of her job, and it will be sent promptly. If you live outside of the United States, check the laws in your area for exemptions.

Is a vegan child less likely to get a disease? One benefit to raising your children on a vegan diet is that you are naturally boosting their immune system. A strong immune system may help your child avoid some of these childhood diseases. But I wouldn't count on a vegan diet to prevent your child from getting chickenpox if he's been playing with a friend who has it.

What About Drugs and Medicines?

Perhaps you're wondering if the ingredients in prescription drugs and life-saving medicines are vegan if the ingredients of vaccines are not vegan. Good question. It is extremely difficult to find a drug that contains no animal products. Also, federal law requires that drugs undergo testing on animals before they can be approved for human use. Even the aspirin you take for a headache is a product of animal cruelty.

So what should you do? If you need a drug to save your life, take it. Until our world is entirely vegan, what choice do you have? Animals need you alive and kicking so you can help free them from their lives of torment. It helps nobody if you're dead because you refused a non-vegan drug that would have saved your life. If you can prevent disease and illness, you won't need drugs and medicine. Prevention is always preferable to treatment. Here are some ways to avoid drugs and medicine.

Boost your immune system naturally. Be sure you and your children are eating plenty of organic, fresh fruits and vegetables that contain vitamins to boost your immune systems. Drink a lot of pure water. Consider using herbs such as Echinacea or Goldenseal, which help boost the immune system. Exercise to release toxins from your body. Seek to provide a stress free environment, stay away from smokers, and try to live in a city with clean air.

Homeopathy. I never really believed homeopathy was effective until I tried it myself. It happened by accident.

I was meeting one of my business clients, Lauren Feder, M.D., to discuss her Web site. Lauren is a medical doctor who specializes in homeopathy with a practice in Beverly Hills, CA. When I arrived at the meeting, I was feeling very ill and nauseated. I believe it was from some questionable food I'd eaten in a hurry on my way to the appointment. Lauren asked me what my symptoms were and gave me a homeopathic remedy. The result was practically instantaneous. My nausea dissipated rapidly and was completely gone in five minutes. She gave me one more dose for good measure. I have to say that I was stunned. I didn't believe it was possible to go from feeling so awful to feeling perfectly fine so fast.

Since discovering homeopathy, I've used it successfully to alleviate symptoms and discomforts from the common cold, and to help my baby when she was teething. If you haven't tried homeopathy yourself, look into it. It's very safe and you can administer it to your babies and children without fear of a bad reaction. Please note that some homeopathic pellets have trace amounts of dairy in them. But if it's a choice between harsh pharmaceuticals with side effects, complications, and risks, or homeopathic medicines, I'll choose homeopathy any day of the week.

Seek alternative treatments. Not all doctors treat illness in the same ways. Some are more prone to prescribe drugs, some recommend surgery, some try to suppress symptoms, and still others recommend letting symptoms run their course. Besides allopathic doctors, you could elect to see a chiropractor, an herbalist, a naturopath, an acupuncturist, or a massage therapist. There are many ways to treat the body. Drugs and medicines are not your only choices.

Avoid taking medicine if you don't really need it. When I got a cold as a child, my mom gave me throat lozenges and a spray for my sore throat, a decongestant tablet for my stuffed up nose, sometimes a nasal spray to shrink swollen nasal membranes, ibuprofen if I had a fever, and cough syrup when I developed a cough. There's one thing they all had in common…they didn't work! Sometimes I had relief of my symptoms for 20 minutes but I'd often end up feeling drowsy or even sick to my stomach.

When I was a child, my colds often lasted weeks and would leave me with a lingering cough that lingered as long as three months. After I went vegan, I stopped getting sick so often and the severity was significantly less. Today, my average cold lasts four days instead of two weeks, is very mild, there's no lingering cough, and my nose is never so stuffed that I can't breathe through it. Compared to illnesses in my youth, this is heaven! Now when I'm sick I don't bother with all those drugs I used to take. Instead, I use steam to clear my nasal passages and deep breathing to clear out my lymph system. I take homeopathic remedies the first 24 hours. I use a eucalyptus rub on my chest and neck to keep my airway open at night. I drink gallons of water, and I suck on natural herbal cough drops. I also stop eating anything refined, or too sugary, and concentrate instead on eating lots of water-rich fruits, soups, and vegetables. Maybe some of these tricks will work for you too. You may not need to take medication at all. For valuable tips and more information about homeopathy from Lauren Feder, M.D., visit www.vegfamily.com/lauren-feder/index.htm.

Chapter 4

FEEDING VEGAN CHILDREN

Now you know that your kids will be the healthiest kids on the block, but what are you going to feed them? How do you make sure they're getting enough calcium, protein, and iron? Are there certain nutrients that are lacking in the vegan diet? Does B_{12} only come from animal products? How will you know if your child has a deficiency? Those are just some of the questions that parents have on their minds when it comes to feeding their vegan kids. But don't worry. By the end of this chapter you'll know how to feed your vegan children and make sure they're getting all their nutrients.

Vitamins, Minerals, and Nutrients
Every parent wants his or her child to eat well, but being vegan doesn't automatically guarantee your child's health. Many parents wonder if they need to make extensive meal plans and keep track of their children's food and vitamin intake. As long as you are certain that your child is eating a varied diet, has a reliable source of $B_{12,}$ and is getting enough calories, sunlight, and essential fatty acids, then you don't need to sit down and plan every meal. I do recommend taking stock of your child's diet occasionally and making sure he's still getting what he needs. If not, make changes, buy different foods, or give him supplements. It's your

responsibility to make sure your child is getting adequate vitamin and mineral intake.

So what do vegan children need to grow up healthy and strong? The following are key vitamins and minerals that vegan parents need to be aware of.

B_{12}. Intake of B_{12} is necessary for synthesis of red blood cells, maintenance of the nervous system, and growth and development in children. Failure to get enough B_{12} in the diet can cause problems like anemia, degeneration of nerve fibers, and irreversible neurological damage.

Today, most people acquire B_{12} from meat, eggs, and dairy products. In order for vegans to get enough B_{12}, they must either supplement the vitamin or eat foods fortified with B_{12}.

Adults who convert to veganism will be able to live off their stores of B_{12} for some time, however vegan infants and children will definitely need a reliable source of B_{12} in their diets. If you're breastfeeding, your baby will get B_{12} from your milk, but only for as long as *you* are getting adequate amounts yourself! At one time, it was believed that algae, seaweed, spirulina, and some soy products were good sources of B_{12}, but as it turns out this is *not* the case. Those are analog forms of B_{12} and do not meet human requirements. In fact, they may interfere with the absorption of real B_{12}. Do not rely on those products for B_{12}.

The recommended daily requirements for B_{12} are as follows:

Age of Child	Daily Requirement
1 to 3	.9 mcg
4 to 8	1.2 mcg
9 to 13	1.8 mcg
14 to 18	2.4 mcg

If you're breastfeeding you need at least 2 micrograms per day. What does a microgram look like? Does it really matter? You don't want to measure it every day anyway. Instead read labels to find foods fortified with B_{12} (cyanocobalamin) and make sure your kids are getting 100% of their daily requirement each day.

The best dietary sources of B_{12} are nutritional yeast (Red Star Vegetarian Support Formula), fortified cereals, fortified soymilk, and fortified juices. B_{12} may also be found in textured vegetable protein (tvp), veggie burger mixes, some margarines, and maybe vegetable stock. Read the labels to know for sure.

If you're not certain your child is getting enough B_{12} from what he eats and drinks, you can give him a vegan multivitamin that contains B_{12}. B_{12} is not considered toxic if you take too much. It is best absorbed in small amounts, though, so try to get 100% each day into your child instead of relying on a once a week dose.

Calcium. Some people believe that only dairy products contain calcium. But that's simply not true. Today it's easy for vegans to get adequate amounts of calcium in their diets. The best food sources for calcium are: tofu (made with calcium carbonate), spinach, dried figs, chickpeas, baked beans, broccoli, almonds, dried apricots, sesame seeds or tahini (sesame butter), and green leafy vegetables (kale, Swiss chard, red leaf lettuce). Also, soymilk and orange juices are often fortified with calcium. You can give your kids calcium supplements, although it's better if they can get their calcium directly from food sources.

Your growing kids require a hefty dose of calcium each day. It could take some initial planning to ensure your children are getting as much as they need. The recommended daily requirements for calcium are as follows:

Age of Child	Daily Requirement
1 to 3	500 mg
4 to 8	800 mg
9 to teen	1300 mg

If you don't habitually serve foods high in calcium, or if your kids reject those foods, then getting that much calcium can be a tall order. That's why I highly recommend the fortified soymilks and juices, since they offer 300 mg of calcium in just one 8 oz serving, an excellent start!

In order for the body to absorb calcium most efficiently, it needs vitamin D. That's why cow's milk is often fortified with vitamin D. So let's turn our attention to this important vitamin.

Vitamin D. Vitamin D is actually not a vitamin at all. It's a hormone our bodies manufacture when our skin is exposed to sunlight. Sufficient vitamin D is necessary to prevent a condition called rickets, which is a softening of the bones. A child needs about 15 minutes per day of sunlight exposure on her arms and face to make sufficient vitamin D. Alternatively, 20 to 30 minutes twice a week will also suffice. Note that sunscreen with SPF 8 or more could inhibit absorption of vitamin D. If your children won't be able to get enough sunlight, then you can supplement their intake with dietary sources of vitamin D (such as soymilk) or with a supplement (use D_2). D_3 is animal derived.

Protein. By a wide margin, protein leads the pack as the number one concern of most people when they find out you and your kids are vegans. But it's actually not that difficult to ensure adequate protein intake. Protein is found in significant amounts in the following foods: whole grains (oats, brown rice, pasta), nuts and seeds (tahini, almond butter, peanut butter), meat analogues, and legumes (tofu, lentils, split peas, garbanzo beans, and beans). It's also found to a lesser degree in vegetables, and yes, even fruit. To ensure adequate protein, be sure your child is not filling up on junk food, refined foods, or empty calories. Include several servings from the legume family each day. Don't let it concern you too much, but occasionally ask yourself if your child is eating foods high in protein, like veggie deli slices, veggie burgers, nuts, nut butters, seeds, legumes, tofu, soymilk, beans, and grains.

Iron. Iron is a definite concern for vegans. It's extremely important that your child's diet contain sufficient quantities of iron. Luckily, however, the vegan diet is rich in foods with high iron content. Plus, vegan diets are extremely high in vitamin C, which increases iron absorption. So with a little planning, you're going to be home free.

Young children from one to three years of age need 12.5 mg of iron each day. Needs increase as a child matures. Females who have begun menstruation need 27 mg of iron each day!

A ½ cup serving of firm tofu will yield 13 mg of iron, and a 1 cup serving of garbanzo beans yields 8 mg of iron. Other foods high in iron include bran flakes, aduki beans, blackstrap molasses, black beans, lentils, pinto beans, soybeans, quinoa, tofu dogs, veggie burgers, pumpkin seeds, tahini, and baked potatoes. Some soymilks are also fortified with iron.

To further increase your child's absorption of iron, be sure to serve those foods listed above with a good source of vitamin C.

Vitamin C. You probably don't need to worry about whether your child is getting enough vitamin C, since intakes in vegans tends to be extremely high. Foods loaded with vitamin C include citrus fruits, strawberries, papaya, mango, guava, kiwi, and cantaloupe. Broccoli, cabbage, tomatoes, peppers, and leafy greens are high in vitamin C. Plus, virtually all commercial fruit juices contain 100% of the RDA for vitamin C. Kids generally love fruit. Try making fruit smoothies in the blender for a treat they'll really love!

For some recipes, visit www.vegfamily.com/vegan-pregnancy/fruit-smoothies.htm.

Zinc. Zinc needs have recently been reduced. Children aged one to three years of age need 3 mg per day. Four to eight-year-olds need 5 mg per day. Nine to thirteen-year-olds need 9 mg per day. And children over thirteen need between 9 and 11 mg per day.

Signs of a zinc deficiency include slow physical growth, poor appetite, and reduced ability to taste. Zinc is vital to the human body and plays a key role in many of the body's systems and processes. Suffice it to say that you don't want your kids to be missing their zinc!

Foods high in zinc include: garbanzo beans, lentils, pinto beans, firm tofu, meat analogue deli slices, almonds, pumpkin seeds, tahini, pecans, pine nuts, and sunflower seeds. Think trail mix (nuts, seeds, and dried fruit) for zinc.

Fiber. Fiber in the diet plays an important role in keeping the body healthy and preventing many major chronic diseases, such as heart disease, cancer, gastrointestinal diseases, diabetes, hypoglycemia, and obesity. Luckily, vegan diets tend to be higher in fiber than vegetarian and meat eating diets.

For children, fiber intake is generally adequate if they are eating a varied, whole foods diet. In this case, avoid giving your children wheat bran, bran muffins, or bran cereal because those foods are too high in fiber and may inhibit mineral absorption. Fruits and vegetables have an abundance of fiber so offer those foods instead. However, if your child is eating a lot of refined, white-flour foods, then a bran muffin will be a welcome addition to his diet.

Essential Fatty Acids

Essential fatty acids (EFAs) get their own category because getting enough EFAs into the diet is extremely important for good vegan health and, unfortunately, it's too often overlooked.

There are two essential fatty acids, omega-6 and omega-3. The good news is that most vegans get enough omega-6 in their diet. The bad news is that most vegans don't get nearly enough omega-3. And to further complicate matters, getting too much omega-6 to the exclusion of omega-3 will prevent your body from forming DHA (docosahexaenoic acid).

In order for the body to make DHA, it must have a good ratio of omega-6 and omega-3 fatty acids. If you're getting too much of one to the exclusion of the other, DHA won't be formed. Low levels of DHA have been associated with depression, schizophrenia, Alzheimer's disease, and Attention Deficit Hyperactivity Disorder (ADHD). In infants, failure to get enough DHA is linked to reduced visual and brain development. The only direct food sources of DHA are fish, eggs, and micro algae.

There are plenty of foods high in omega-6 fatty acids, and you probably eat them in abundance, for example corn oil, safflower oil, sunflower oil, walnuts, tofu and other soy products. However, foods that are high in omega-3 fatty acids are less likely to find their way into vegan diets. The foods highest in omega-3s are flaxseed oil, hempseed oil, walnut oil, canola oil soybean oil, flaxseeds (whole and ground), walnuts and butternuts, and green leafy vegetables.

These foods are not usually abundant in a person's diet, so what are you going to do? My advice is to begin with flaxseeds. Flax oil is sold in health food stores, although it is usually quite expensive. You can put flax oil in smoothies, yogurt, mashed potatoes, salad dressings, cereals, and in anything else where the taste will not be that noticeable. However, flax oil is damaged by excessive heat so don't cook with it.

Flaxseeds have a shell around them so are less likely to be damaged from heat, but once they're ground, they are no longer protected. Buy some whole flaxseeds in your health food store and use them when you bake (grind them).

You can even use flaxseeds as an egg replacer by combining one tablespoon of ground flax seeds with three tablespoons of water or other liquid, and then use this in place of eggs in a recipe when you bake.

Consider using walnuts when you bake, as they are high in omega-3 fatty acids as well. Let your children eat raw walnuts if they aren't allergic to them.

DHA supplements are now available in veggie caps, but may be hard to locate. If you can only find DHA supplements in gel caps, you can open the cap and squeeze the DHA onto your tongue or put it into food. The bottom line on these essential fatty acids is: don't ignore them. Be certain your child has a reliable source of omega-6 and omega-3 fatty acids.

Children aged one to three years of age need 1.1 grams of omega-3 fatty acids per day. A teaspoon of flax oil per day should be sufficient.

The Picky Eater

You're a conscientious parent. You've studied which foods are high in essential vitamins, made a list of recipes that include those foods, gone shopping, and slaved away in the kitchen all day to make the perfect vegan dinner. Your family sits down to a meal that consists of: tofu nut loaf, steamed veggies (broccoli, spinach, and kale), macaroni and cheese (made with a nutritional yeast sauce), salad with flax oil dressing, and whole wheat dinner rolls; a cornucopia of vitamins and minerals! Your spouse eyes it suspiciously but likes to try new things. Your nine-year-old scrunches up his nose and says, "Eww, what *is* this stuff?" You explain what you're eating and he says, "I don't like tofu, this sauce smells funny, I want white bread, and you know I hate broccoli!" He pushes his plate away. You start to worry because all he's had to eat all day is a peanut butter and jelly sandwich and an oatmeal cookie. What do you do when you have a finicky toddler, adolescent, or teen who won't even try the healthy foods you're bringing into his life? Whether your picky child is two years old or seventeen here are some tried and true techniques to get your children past the picky stage.

Count to ten. Studies show that it can take up to ten encounters with a new food before your young child will like it. So just because your child rejects the food once, it doesn't mean you need to stop trying with that food. Wait a week and try again, and again. I remember when I first fed Emily peas. She spit them out. I stopped buying peas for a while. But one day I was feeding her vegetable soup that contained peas. She thought they were so cute. She kept picking out the peas, talking to them and popping them in her mouth, laughing. So I started bringing peas back into her life and now she loves them.

Prepare the food differently. If your child rejects a food, try preparing it a little differently. For example, maybe your child finds tofu cubes a little too squishy and flavorless. Try blending soft tofu in a blender and using it in place of eggs and milk in a pumpkin pie. Or use blended tofu in baked goods. Your child may never notice. Or switch to firm tofu, cut into strips, dredged in whole-wheat flour and nutritional yeast, and pan-fried. Give your child a dip like barbecue sauce, sweet and sour sauce, or even ketchup. I haven't met a child yet who didn't like ketchup.

Hide healthy foods in old favorites. Does your child hate vegetables? Sneak them into other foods so she doesn't know she's eating them. For example, you can put diced or pureed zucchini, broccoli, mushrooms, or spinach in her favorite tomato sauce and use it in lasagna or over spaghetti. She probably won't notice. How about making sweet breads like pumpkin-walnut or banana bread? Some kids don't like raw fruit, but if you blend it with juice and frozen strawberries, pour it in a glass, and give them a straw, they may surprise you by how fast they gulp it down.

Limit snacking, especially before meals. If your child isn't hungry at dinnertime it's easy to reject new foods that aren't palate pleasers. Make sure your child is not full on juice or too many in-between meal snacks when you serve new foods. A hungry child is more likely to try something new than one with a full belly.

Serve new foods alongside old favorites. The whole meal doesn't have to be made up entirely of new foods. Serve some of his favorites alongside a new recipe, and give your child a chance to adopt the new food into his repertoire. Soon that new food will be an accepted old food.

You can also add new foods to old favorites. For example, if your child likes to eat vegetable stir-fries try adding a little tofu in with it, or sprinkle some nutritional yeast on it just before serving, or make a new sweet and sour sauce that contains pineapple.

Make the food attractive. Make sure the new foods you're introducing are attractively presented. Plain white cubes of steamed tofu aren't that appealing to people who are new to tofu (or even people who like tofu). Instead of serving one vegetable, serve a medley of multi-colored veggies like corn with red peppers, black beans, and green beans. Add colorful veggies to rice. Serve fruit salad instead of just cut up cantaloupe. And for the little ones, have some fun making their buckwheat pancakes look like cute animals using raisins for the eyes, a strawberry for the nose, and a piece of melon in the shape of a smile.

Let your kids help. Kids are more likely to eat foods that they helped make, so let them pick recipes, go shopping with you, and help prepare the dish when you get home. Be sure to compliment them on their excellent choice of a recipe!

Vegan Cooking

Maybe you're a gourmet chef able to concoct new recipes without a glimmer of hesitation, or maybe you're grateful if you can open a box, boil water, or get the lid off a can of soup. Whatever your culinary skills, your kids have to eat, and you have to provide them with healthy, nutritious food. What are you going to do? Where will you get recipes? What foods taste good with what? What do you do with nutritional yeast and flax oil? What's the difference between soft and firm tofu? And what is a mung bean anyway?

Get vegan cookbooks. Vegan cookbooks are great for learning how to make delicious vegan recipes. After all, someone's already done the hard part of concocting, tasting, and testing. All you have to do is follow the recipe. Plus, vegan cookbooks usually contain valuable information besides just recipes. From cookbooks you can learn about new foods, what they're used for, where to buy them, and how to tell if they are in season. Cookbooks often contain nutritional information as well. For a list of recommended vegan cookbooks, see www.vegfamily.com/book-reviews/index.htm.

Develop your own recipes. If you're a culinary genius, or simply a creative person, why not develop your own recipes. I have friends who understand exactly how different ingredients will affect a recipe. They seem to know when to use baking soda versus baking powder or when to use flax "eggs" versus egg replacer. Once you've become familiar with the subtleties of vegan cooking, you'll probably have an inner sense about substitutions as well. And remember, you don't have use fake ground beef to make tacos, you can make bean tacos instead.

Veganize your old favorites. Don't throw out those old cookbooks so fast! I've had a great deal of success turning recipes from my old cookbooks into vegan masterpieces simply by substituting ingredients. Usually the dessert section and the side dish sections of my old cookbooks are easily turned vegan with just a few substitutions. Plus, you might be surprised to find a few vegan recipes lurking inside those old cookbooks.

Browse the health food stores. To get ideas for new recipes, spend some time browsing slowly through your local health food store. When I first did this, I discovered a whole new world of food waiting for me of which I had no previous knowledge. I found natural sodas, grains I'd never heard of (like quinoa and millet), red leaf lettuce, date sugar, pure maple syrup, egg replacer, seaweed, brown rice crackers, umeboshi paste, and curry to name just a few. It wasn't long before these new foods found their way into my meals and adopted a permanent place in my kitchen.

Don't give up. Don't give up on a recipe just because it didn't come out right the first time you tried it. I had an old pancake recipe that called for eggs and I used tofu instead. It didn't come out right, so I tried using egg replacer and that turned out a little better. Then a friend told me that if I'm only replacing one egg in a recipe to just use water. I tried that and the pancakes came out perfectly! It may take you some experimenting to get a recipe just right.

Substitutions Guide

If you're new to vegan cooking you may be looking for substitutions you can use in your old non-vegan recipes. Thankfully, there are plenty of products vegans can use in place of animal ingredients that will make vegan cooking a breeze. Let's cover how to replace animal ingredients with vegan ingredients.

Milk. It's very easy to substitute for cow's milk in a recipe. You can use soymilk, rice milk, oat milk, or nut milk measure for measure. To make buttermilk, put 1 tablespoon of vinegar or lemon juice in your measuring cup and then add your soymilk to the amount specified in the recipe.

Cheese. Vegan cheeses do exist, although they don't all taste good, not all of them melt, and they are somewhat difficult to find. Be sure to read the label as some vegetarian cheeses contain casein, which is not vegan. If you can find a great vegan cheese that you like, use it in your recipes in the same manner that you would use dairy cheese.

If you need to make a melted cheese sauce, get the Uncheese Cookbook by Joanne Stepaniak for a plethora of "cheesy" recipes using nutritional yeast (which is high in B_{12}). Or see www.vegfamily.com/product-reviews/index.htm for a list of vegan cheeses and other cheese-like products.

In place of cottage or ricotta cheese, you can use crumbled tofu, but remember that it won't melt or have the same creamy consistency you'd expect from cottage or ricotta cheese. You may need to spice it up with herbs and add some salt to make it work in your recipe.

Eggs. A great substitute for scrambled eggs is tofu scramble. You can either use a recipe from a cookbook or simply buy a box of Tofu Scrambler in the store that you then mix with crumbled tofu and heat in a frying pan. Kids generally like tofu scramble, especially kids who have been vegan their entire lives. You can spice it up with tomatoes, peppers, onions, or even potatoes and vegan bacon bits.

In baked goods, good substitutions for eggs include applesauce, pureed soft tofu, Ener-G egg replacer, a flax egg (1 tablespoon ground flax seeds plus 3 tablespoons water or other liquid, blended), or mashed bananas. You'll have to experiment with your recipe to see what works best for you.

In dishes where eggs are usually used for binding (such as meatloaf) you can use oat or soy flour, rolled oats, cooked oatmeal, bread crumbs, instant potato flakes, nut butters, tomato paste, or cornstarch.

For glazing pie crust or phyllo dough with egg wash, just use soymilk instead.

Beef or chicken stock. Replace beef or chicken stock with water or vegetable broth. Or use vegetable bouillon cubes.

Butter. There are vegan margarines on the market that work well in substituting for butter. Be sure to read the labels because not all margarines are vegan. You may also want to consider using oils like canola, sunflower, olive or corn instead of butter or margarine.

Yogurt. Several companies make soy yogurts that will substitute well in your recipes. You can find them in fruit flavors and also plain for cooking and baking.

Sour Cream. Try plain soy yogurt, especially if used in making dips. There are also a few commercially available vegan sour creams on the market. In addition, there are several vegan cookbooks that have excellent recipes for vegan sour cream in them.

Mayonnaise. There are a few vegan mayonnaise products on the market. You can use vegan mayonnaise exactly the way you'd use the non-vegan mayonnaise. Vegan cookbooks often contain a recipe for vegan mayonnaise as well; I've made at least two recipes from cookbooks that came out better than the real thing!

Gelatin. If you need to substitute for gelatin in a recipe, use agar flakes or powder. It will thicken as it is heated. Also, there are a couple of companies that make a vegan fruit gelatin product that you should be able to find at your local health food market.

Honey. There are many liquid sweeteners on the market that you can use in your recipes instead of honey. However, they all vary in consistency and sweetness, making substitution a guessing game, at least initially. You may have to experiment with ratios until you figure out what works best in your recipes.

In general, however, maple syrup and liquid FruitSource can be substituted measure for measure in recipes. Other sweeteners that are less sweet than honey include agave syrup, corn syrup, malt syrup, light and dark molasses, and brown rice syrup. Frozen fruit-juice concentrates, sorghum syrup, and concentrated fruit syrups range from being half as sweet to just as sweet as honey.

Sugar. Many vegans do not eat sugar since some sugar is refined using bone char from animals. Others object to using sugar simply because it isn't as healthy as other sweeteners, it's often full of pesticides, and the sugar plantation workers aren't always treated very well. If you want to replace crystalline sugar in a recipe, here are some alternatives: beet sugar, fructose, organic sugar, unbleached cane sugar, turbinado sugar, date sugar, maple crystals, and granulated FruitSource. Some of these sugars dissolve better than others, so again, you'll have to experiment.

Chocolate. I'm sure there are many people who simply could not be vegan if it meant giving up chocolate, but luckily they don't have to. There are non-dairy vegan chocolate chips, cocoa powders, and chocolate bars that are easily found in the health food store. Be warned that some brands of non-dairy chocolate chips don't melt too well in a cookie. You can also switch to using carob (powder and chips) instead of chocolate in your recipes.

Meat. If you want your foods to have a similar taste and texture to meat, you're in luck, because never before have so many companies manufactured products just for us. Among the products on the market now that will substitute for meat are: veggie deli slices (bologna, ham, turkey, and other flavors), veggie burgers, veggie meatballs, veggie sausage links and patties, veggie bacon, veggie ground "beef," soy chicken patties and nuggets, veggie meatloaf and Salisbury steak, veggie jerky, and whole "turkeys" for Thanksgiving or other holidays.

Check your vegan cookbooks for recipes for foods like "neatloaf," nut roasts, lentil-walnut pates, and other old favorites that traditionally contained animal flesh.

Ice Cream. Along with the proliferation of meat analogues, your health food store is now probably well stocked with vegan ice cream. This industry has grown tremendously from the day I first went vegan. There are vegan ice creams with a soy base, rice base, or nut base, and they're all delicious. Some are high in fat and some are fat-free. Some are fruity like sorbet, while others are sinfully decadent like butter pecan, peanut butter zig-zag, or peanut caramel. You can also buy vegan ice cream sandwiches, mud pies, and ice cream bars. I've made some great shakes, floats, and malts using vegan ice cream products. Your kids will love them too!

Dining Out

People often wonder how hard it is to eat out when you're vegan. It's not hard once you get the hang of it, but in the beginning there are indeed challenges. You have to wonder if the rice you just ordered contains chicken stock, or if the beans you're staring at were made with lard. So what do vegans do to ensure that the food they're getting is really vegan?

Start looking around for vegan or vegetarian restaurants in your city. Ask at your health food store if anyone knows of some good vegetarian restaurants in the area. In fact, I discovered a fantastic, entirely vegan Chinese restaurant in my area when I happened to get into a conversation with another shopper at my supermarket. Before I left the parking lot, I had a menu from the restaurant, and was plotting my first take out order. We're now regular patrons of that restaurant. Once you find a vegan or vegetarian restaurant, strive to give them most of your dining out dollars since you'll be supporting people who may even be vegan themselves. You don't want your only veg restaurant to disappear for lack of business!

If there aren't any vegan restaurants in your area, don't despair. With a little creativity, some planning, and a lot of questions, you'll soon be eating vegan at just about any restaurant in town. Following is a guide for successfully finding vegan fare at non-vegetarian restaurants.

Scan the menu for the vegetarian section. I guess it depends on where you live, but here in Los Angeles when you open up a menu there is often a section just for vegetarians. That's where to begin your search. Some of the options will have cheese in them, but ask if the chef can leave it out. You'll probably at least find a steamed vegetable with rice entree.

Look at side dishes. If the menu doesn't have a vegetarian section, try looking at the side dishes. Often you can get a baked potato, french fries, fruit cup, beans, vegetable of the day, steamed vegetables, or rice. You can make a whole meal with side dishes if you're at the right restaurant.

Salads. Salads are a good bet too. Salads that are traditionally served with meat often taste fine without the meat. For example, try a Chinese chicken salad with no chicken. Check to make sure the dressing is vegan. Salads have become meals in and of themselves. You can usually find salad at a restaurant; it's just a question of getting a vegan dressing. If the dressing isn't vegan you can try requesting oil and vinegar, since most restaurants will have that available. If you like the salad at a certain restaurant but they don't have vegan dressing, bring some of your own in a plastic container.

Watch out for the bread. When your server brings bread to the table, even if it looks vegan, it may have milk in it. Ask your server if the bread contains butter, milk, whey, or eggs. In my experience, most restaurants do *not* bring vegan bread to the table.

Concoct your own meal. Often I will scan a menu for ingredients and ask my server to make something special for me using ingredients on the menu. For example, even if a restaurant does not serve a veggie sandwich, if I notice that they have avocado, lettuce, tomato, and onions, I will have them make me a sandwich using those ingredients. I sometimes add mustard when they bring it to the table or sometimes they'll add it for me. Make sure the bread they're using is vegan. Usually sourdough or rye is safe.

Ask detailed questions. It can be somewhat annoying to ask detailed questions like: what's in the bread, what's in the dressing, does the veggie burger have cheese or eggs in it, do the beans have lard, or does the rice have chicken stock. Still, it's very important, and you only have to do it once. After you're familiar with the fare at a particular restaurant, you can be reasonably confident that it will be made the same way the next time you order it. Every few months ask the same questions in case the recipes have changed.

Contact the company's Web site for information. When I'm headed to a new restaurant, I usually try to find their Web site online first so I can scan the menu. If they don't have a Web site, I'll call the restaurant and ask them what items on their menu would be suitable for vegans. One major chain restaurant I contacted said they did not cater to vegetarians or vegans at all since only 1% of their business comes from that group. They were uninterested in making any attempt to accommodate me and have never had my business since! Another large restaurant chain had a different reaction. They not only answered my emailed question within five minutes, but also made a special effort to tell me how to order vegan in their restaurant. That's a restaurant I go to frequently, and it's popular with my non-vegan friends too, so everyone is happy.

Ask your server for a recommendation. Sometimes asking your server for a recommendation will get you a very special meal. Once while dining at a Chinese restaurant, we were having trouble finding foods that didn't have meat products in them. Our waiter took note of all our questions and asked if we were vegans. We told him we were, and he told us that the chef had three vegan dishes in his arsenal that he could make us. These items were not on the menu and we never would have thought to ask for them. All three dishes were delicious and now every time we go there we get our special meals.

Kid fare. What are the most common items on a kid's menu? Hamburgers, hot dogs, grilled cheese sandwiches, spaghetti and meatballs, chicken fingers, and peanut butter and jelly. That doesn't give you much room for maneuvering. Skip the kid's menu if you can't find anything vegan, and see if they'll make a child-size portion of something from the regular menu.

Fast food. Is there anything vegan at fast food restaurants? Yes, but it's hard to find. If you're in a pinch and need to eat at a fast food restaurant, here are some recommendations:

- French fries (but make sure they aren't made with animal flavorings or oils)
- Plain baked potato
- Sub sandwich with no mayonnaise or cheese (check the bread!)
- Bean burrito without cheese and sour cream
- Tostada salad with beans, and no cheese or sour cream
- Salads with an Italian or oil and vinegar dressing

Sometimes you can find onion rings, veggie burgers, or veggie wraps that are vegan, if you're lucky.

Foods to look for. The following are examples of the kind of foods you'll probably be able to find or concoct when dining in non-vegan restaurants.

- Steamed or grilled vegetables
- Steamed rice with tamari or soy sauce
- Spaghetti with marinara sauce
- Veggie pizza with no cheese
- Chinese chicken salad with no chicken
- Veggie sandwich on sourdough or rye bread
- Fruit plate
- Falafel sandwich (make sure there's no eggs or yogurt in it)
- Toast with jelly
- Baked potatoes

- French fries
- Veggie burgers

What's For Dinner?

My aunt threw a baby shower for me when I was pregnant with my daughter, Emily. My aunt decided to serve chicken, cheese lasagna, salad, and garlic bread. I opted to bring my own meal entirely. When it was time for lunch, people saw that my plate was empty and I could read the look on their faces, "Poor pregnant vegan girl has nothing to eat – what a restrictive diet." Little did they know, I was using the microwave to reheat the leftovers I'd brought. When my meal arrived at the table, delicious smells wafted under the noses of people eating rubber chicken. Someone asked, "What do you have there, Erin? It smells so good." And I said, "Potato lentil stew, curried chickpeas, green beans in a peanut sauce, baked sweet potato, salad with creamy garlic dressing, and sourdough bread with roasted red pepper hummus." People looked from their plate to mine and back again and I knew their pity had been replaced by envy. I'm relating this story so you'll know that being vegan doesn't mean deprivation. Being vegan means eating fresh, delicious, scrumptious food that doesn't cost the life of an innocent animal.

To give you an idea of the variety of food you could be eating and serving to your families, following is a list of many of the foods that my husband, daughter, and I eat on a regular basis. I'm sure your family will have their own favorites!

Breakfast

- Whole grain pancakes with pure maple syrup
- Blueberry waffles with pure maple syrup
- Soy flax waffles with pure maple syrup
- French toast with syrup and vegan powdered sugar

- Whole-wheat toast with margarine and fruit preserves
- Cereal with soymilk
- Muffins (banana nut, pumpkin, apple, blueberry)
- Fruit smoothies
- Fresh fruit
- Apple cinnamon oatmeal
- Maple oatmeal with raisins
- Tofu scramble
- Potatoes with onions and red and green peppers
- Bagels with vegan cream cheese
- Veggie sausage links
- Vegan bacon
- Soy yogurt

Lunch

- Veggie sandwich (lettuce, tomato, onions, and avocado)
- Club sandwich (vegan bacon bits and veggie deli slices)
- Peanut butter and jelly sandwich
- Garden salad with Thousand Island dressing,
- Mock "chicken" salad (tofu, Vegenaise, celery, onions)
- Black beans with barbecue sauce
- Veggie burgers (lettuce, tomato, ketchup, and mustard)
- Split pea soup
- Fresh vegetable soup
- Baked potato (margarine, vegan sour cream)
- Rice cakes (hummus, red pepper, tomato, black pepper)
- Veggie deli slice sandwich (vegan mayo, lettuce, tomato)

- Falafel sandwich (pita bread, hummus, tomato, cucumber)
- French fries (baked or deep fried)

Snacks

- Tortilla chips with salsa and/or guacamole
- Popcorn with melted margarine or nutritional yeast
- Celery sticks with creamy garlic dressing or peanut butter
- Carrot sticks with dressing
- Trail mix
- Cashews
- Walnuts
- Dried apricots
- Dates
- Fresh fruit
- Potato chips
- Soy crisps
- Fruit leather

Dinner

- Vegetable pot pie
- Baked sweet potatoes
- Mashed potatoes with vegan gravy
- Corn on the cob
- Green beans in a peanut sauce
- Chickpea casserole
- Curried chickpeas
- Potato lentil stew
- Turkish stew
- Split pea and vegetable stew
- Black bean and corn enchiladas

- Bean burritos with guacamole, rice, lettuce, and salsa
- Steamed broccoli and squash with fresh ginger and tamari
- Vegetable stir-fry with sweet and sour sauce,
- Vegan egg rolls
- Spaghetti with marinara sauce and veggie meatballs
- Spinach lasagna with tofu cheese
- Veggie pizzas with vegan mozzarella
- Tempeh "fish" sandwich with vegan tartar sauce
- Chinese chicken salad without the chicken,
- Roasted vegetable quesadillas with vegan cheese
- Portabella mushroom burgers
- Vegan "ribs" with barbecue sauce
- Veggie meatloaf

Dessert
- Cookies (online, homemade, or store-bought)
- Pies (apple, pumpkin, cashew cream, strawberry)
- Cakes (from mixes or store-bought)
- Chocolate (bars, fudge, chips)
- Donuts
- Candies
- Ice cream (bars, cones, pies)
- Peanut butter rice crispy treats

As you can see, there is a tremendous amount of variety in the vegan diet. Share some of your favorite vegan meals with your non-vegan friends and family members and watch them open their minds to the possibilities of being vegan. My non-vegan family members are generally surprised by how good our food tastes. My mother deeply appreciates it when my husband and I cook for her. She's never once complained that the food was unusual. As she says, "If this is how you guys eat all the time, I could be a vegan."

For more articles and information about nutrition for your vegan children, see:
www.vegfamily.com/babies-and-toddlers/index.htm
www.vegfamily.com/vegan-children/index.htm
www.vegfamily.com/articles/index.htm

Chapter 5

SCHOOLS AND DAYCARE

When your children are young, it's easy to supervise what they're eating. You are in charge of buying their food and probably preparing it as well. But someday your child will go off to school, go out with friends, be invited to parties, and you'll have to trust that she will make the right decisions. The tools, knowledge, confidence, and wisdom that you give her will help her to make the choices you'd like her to make.

When it comes time to place your child in daycare or send her off to school, you must make sure that there's a system in place to handle her dietary needs. Will the staff or teacher remember that your child is a vegan and make sure that she doesn't eat anything non-vegan? Is there something you can do to ensure that your child is fed only vegan meals while away from you? How will you handle accidents, unexpected classroom parties, field trips, and candy drives? Will your child ever be able to eat in the cafeteria with the other children? Will your child be asked to do something that goes against his vegan values, such as dissecting an animal in biology class? Will your child be teased for being vegan and, if so, how will you help him deal with it?

It can be difficult for any parent to watch her child go out into the world for the first time, seemingly unprotected.

There are even more challenges for vegan parents. But with a little preparation and forethought, you can prevent or easily handle situations that will invariably come your way.

Daycare Centers

There are several important factors to consider when looking for a daycare center for your child. You want to be sure the staff-to-child ratio is small, the facility is clean, the staff is experienced and friendly, the center is licensed, and the hours fit your schedule and needs. Because you're a vegan you also want to know how meals are handled. Does the center provide a meal or snack? Will there be a vegan option? Will you be charged for meals even if you end up having to provide foods for your vegan child? How will the staff ensure that your child isn't accidentally given something non-vegan? Will new staff be informed of your child's diet?

Following are some tips to help you find a daycare center and ensure that your child gets vegan meals and snacks while he's there. We'll also discuss how to handle problems that may arise.

Ask around for referrals. There could be a great, vegan-friendly daycare in your area and you may not even know about it. Go to vegetarian potlucks, health food stores, and food co-ops and strike up a conversation with other parents to see if they know of a vegan-friendly daycare center. Begin looking at those centers. If none of them are suitable, just go through your local phone book to find other daycare centers in your area. Ask the staff about their policies regarding children with special dietary needs, and pick the center that's best suited to work with you.

Find a veg-friendly daycare center. Wouldn't it be wonderful if there were vegan daycare centers? Unfortunately, the demand in any given area is likely to be small; thus the chance is remote that an all-vegan daycare center could stay in business very long. However, you might be able to find a vegetarian daycare center where, at the very least, the staff would be respectful of kids with special dietary needs. If you can find one, great! If not, find the best daycare center you can and work to make the situation as close to perfect as possible.

Educate the staff. The first thing you must do after you've picked a daycare center is to educate the staff who will be there when your child is there. When you sit down to fill out forms, write your check, or listen to their sales pitch, bring up the fact that your child is vegan and ask them how they handle kids with dietary restrictions. If they are vague, don't have a precedent, or don't seem concerned, take that as a bad sign. There should be a system in place to deal with kids with dietary restrictions and food allergies. If not, find another center. If you get a good response and it sounds like they'll be able to honor your wishes, go ahead with your plan to put your child in their care.

Next, provide documentation that states your wishes that your child be served only vegan foods while at the center. Make a list of foods your child can eat and foods that he can't. Reassure them that you will be available to answer questions if the staff is unsure whether an item is vegan. Be friendly and informative, not dictating and demanding. However, make it clear to the owner that you will remove your child from the center if you find out the staff has *purposely* given your child something non-vegan to eat, and that you will expect a refund of your remaining tuition. As long as you have been straightforward, and they have agreed to your requests, you have every right to expect them to follow your rules governing what to feed your child.

Should you lie? Some parents will tell their daycare centers that their children are allergic to certain foods, or that they are not allowed to have meat, dairy, and eggs. Many parents feel this is easier and less intimidating than explaining veganism. They also think the staff will be more likely to comply with their request because, as in the case of allergies, it's a matter of life and death. I don't recommend lying, however. If you believe that the only way to get the staff to agree with your request is to lie to them, then what does that say about the staff and the center? You have to be able to trust these people; they're taking care of your child. Besides, how would the staff feel if and when they found out that your child is a vegan and that you lied to them? They may not take your request as seriously as they used to. So instead of lying, become comfortable educating people about veganism. You have nothing to apologize for. If you tell the truth, the center may start carrying more fruits and vegetables to serve as snacks, which will benefit all of the children, not just your own.

Make it easy on the caregivers. Daycare center employees are human, and they can make a mistake. It's your job to make sure that it's as easy on the staff as possible to give your child only vegan foods. There are several things you can do to ensure success for everyone.

First, consider putting a cute pin on your child's backpack or clothing that says, "I'm vegan. No meat, dairy, eggs, or honey for me please!" Or, put a piece of masking tape on your child's clothing each morning that says, "I'm vegan!" so the staff can see it clearly.

Second, stock some pre-packaged snacks at the center for emergencies. Many parents send soymilk or juice boxes, cookies, applesauce, fruit leather, and other non-perishable items that the staff can grab at a moment's notice. You may even prefer to supply all of your child's meals because it could be preferable to letting the staff make decisions while they're trying to feed 30 hungry kids.

Third, make a food list. In one column, list items that your child can eat, and in the other column, list foods your child cannot eat. Ask the staff what they are feeding the other children, go through those items, and check which ones your child can and cannot eat. Make sure those foods are on the list in the appropriate columns. Ask them to store the list close to their refrigerator or on a cupboard so they can see it easily.

Note the employee turnover rate. Turnover rates in daycare centers are generally high, with new employees coming in every three to six months. You must be certain that new staff members are educated about your child's dietary needs. When you drop off your child and notice a new staff member, introduce yourself and work into the conversation that your child is a vegan. "I'm not sure if they told you already or not, but my child is a vegan and can't eat meat, eggs, or dairy products. There's a list over there (point to it) of foods she can have, and I've left a stash of food here in this cupboard if she ever needs it. Whatever you do, please do not let my child eat any meat, eggs, or dairy products."

Show your appreciation. Everyone likes to receive compliments. If you feel the staff is doing a great job be sure to thank them occasionally so they know their efforts have not gone unnoticed. You can even bring them a fruit basket, or some delicious vegan cookies to show your appreciation!

Handle problems quickly. If you find out that your child ate something non-vegan, you have to find out what happened and make sure it won't happen again.

First, get the details of the situation. Was it a new employee who simply didn't know? Did your child take food from another child's plate? Did someone forget to read the ingredients? Was there an unexpected birthday party and your child just grabbed a piece of cake without realizing it wasn't vegan?

Second, make sure it won't happen again. That could mean educating a new employee, instructing your child not to take food from other children's plates, asking the staff to keep a closer eye on your child, having the staff feed your child first, and/or reminding the staff to check ingredients and refer to your list. In the case of unexpected birthday cake or other treats, be sure you've got some vegan goodies stashed there so that the staff can give them to your child while everyone else is eating non-vegan treats.

Third, tell the director of the daycare center what happened so that he can take whatever appropriate action may be warranted. If there is an employee who is willfully giving your child non-vegan food because she doesn't care about, or agree with, your dietary restrictions, it will behoove you to get the owner involved. Either the employee will have to change her ways, be dismissed, be moved to a different shift, or you will have to take your child out of that daycare center.

Form your own daycare or babysitting co-op. If you can find enough vegan parents, you may be able to arrange to have one of the parents take care of all of them. Caregiver to child ratio rules still apply, however; don't saddle one person with too many kids of varying ages. The parents can either contribute money for food and supplies or bring them in. You should also pay the primary caregiver and the helpers a salary. This may not be a good long-term option, so be prepared to look for a daycare center again if you have to.

Hire a nanny or babysitter. Another option is to hire a nanny to come to your home. The benefits of having someone come to your home are enormous. For one, all the food in your home is vegan, so no matter what the nanny selects from the refrigerator, you know it will be safe. Your child will be sick less often since he won't be around other kids. You won't have to worry about accidents, unexpected parties, or disrespectful staff. Hiring a nanny will probably be a more expensive option than putting your child in daycare, but it might be worth it to you. While your child is napping at home, perhaps the nanny can double as a housekeeper or make dinner for you. Your nanny does not have to be a vegan herself, but she does need to respect your vegan values.

Selecting a School

Wouldn't it be great if all schools were vegan? There'd be vegan food in the cafeteria, the vending machines would be full of fruit and carrot sticks, the drink machines would offer soymilk and juice, fundraisers would involve selling vegan cookies or vegan candy, Earth Day would be celebrated with pomp and ceremony, students would plant gardens and take care of animals, and there would be recycling bins instead of trash cans located throughout the schoolyard. Kids wouldn't be teased or bullied, there would be no dissection of animals in biology classes, and field trips would be to animal rescues instead of zoos. It's a nice dream, isn't it? Unfortunately, today this dream is far from reality, and we have to make due with the few options available.

When it comes time to select a school for your child, you have three options: homeschooling, private, or public. Here are the benefits and drawbacks of each option.

Homeschool. Homeschooling is becoming more popular among parents who are unhappy with the current state of education. If you decide to homeschool your child he will benefit from the ease of maintaining a vegan environment, and he probably won't get sick as often. Just make sure you're not using homeschooling as an excuse to avoid putting your child in a public situation with non-vegan children. Eventually he'll have to learn how to deal with being a vegan in a world that isn't vegan.

There are a few drawbacks to homeschooling. One of the drawbacks is that it is time consuming; you or your partner will have to set aside several hours each day to homeschool your child, prepare lessons, and make sure that your child is learning at an appropriate rate. You also need to be fairly well educated to ensure that your child is getting a well-rounded education, especially at higher grade levels. For example, are you fluent in a foreign language? Can you teach your child algebra or trigonometry?

Private school. If you choose to send your child to a private school, you will at least have the opportunity to shop around for the best environment for your child. Since many private schools are founded on alternative principles, staff and teachers may be more open and accepting of your lifestyle. Private schools don't rely on funding from the government as much as public schools, so you may have some luck convincing the cafeteria to serve more vegan options than you would at a public school. The drawback to private schools are the price and the fact that often your child's school friends may not live nearby so it will be harder for them to get together for play.

Public school. If you send your child to the local public school, you'll have to take what you get. Because public schools rely heavily on federal funding for their school lunch programs, it may be next to impossible to get vegan or even vegetarian options on the menu. You'll probably have to pack your child's lunch on all or most occasions. Staff and teachers may be less open to your lifestyle, and you may meet more resistance when you suggest that they do things that are new to normal school practices. The more involved you are in helping out at the school, the better. Later in this chapter we'll discuss ways to get involved and make a difference in your child's school. The benefits to public school are that your kids will learn early on how to handle themselves in non-vegan environments, their friends will live nearby, and the price for schooling is, of course, already paid out of your tax contributions.

Principals, Teachers, and Staff

If you've enrolled your child in public or private school, you'll want to make sure that his needs will be taken care of. That means explaining his dietary stipulations to his teacher and school principal. But how should you do that?

Make an appointment. Don't go up to the teacher on the first day of school and mention, in passing, that your child is a vegan. The teacher will probably be a little distracted and may not fully understand what you're telling her. A week before school starts, call the school's office, find out who your child's teacher is going to be, and ask if you can speak to the teacher and/or principal about a matter that is very important to you. Tell them it won't take more than 20 minutes of their time and that you would really appreciate it.

If for some reason you can't get an appointment, ask for the teacher to give you a call at home before the school year starts. Or, see if the teacher will be in her classroom the day before school starts. Teachers often get their classrooms ready, so you have a good chance of catching her when she's alone and has some time for you.

If all else fails, when you pick up your child on the first day of school, wait until everyone else has gone and ask the teacher if she can spare ten minutes to discuss your child's special needs. Whatever happens, at some point you will need to have a conversation with your child's teacher, and most likely the principal as well. Don't put it off indefinitely and don't wait too long.

Do your homework. Before you go to the meeting, make a checklist of all the things you want to talk about so you can keep the meeting brief and to the point. Bring the list of foods your child can and cannot eat, and give a copy to the teacher and one to the principal for inclusion in your child's file. Tell them how you want field trips, fundraisers, and parties handled. If you have a doctor's note that your child is to be served calcium fortified orange juice or soymilk instead of cow's milk for lunch, bring copies of that for the principal, teacher, and cafeteria manager. Be sure to keep a copy for yourself.

Make it easy on them. Provide the teacher with as much help as possible. Teachers have as many as 30 kids in a classroom, and they can't be expected to give your child more attention than the other kids. As soon as possible, bring in a box full of non-perishable snacks to store in the teacher's classroom. Then, in a pinch (i.e., your child forgot his lunch or someone brought in a birthday cake), the teacher can give your child items from the stash. You don't want your child to endure sitting there with nothing to eat in those situations. Items to put in the special box can include: fruit leather, vegan cookies, candies, donuts, potato chips, juice boxes, soymilk boxes, crackers, applesauce, nuts, and raisins. If you can easily afford it, supply extra treats for the other kids in the class so your child is not the only one eating something different. Be sure to get the teacher's permission to leave this food in the classroom. You don't want to just barge in and start putting food in her cupboards. Also, be sure she keeps the food out of reach and out of sight of the other children so someone else does not eat it by mistake.

> **Real Stories from Real Parents:**
> *The teacher tells me that my daughter asks for a vegan alternative [when non-vegan foods are being supplied to the children] because she "is a vegan and shouldn't eat such things." –* Chandra

Be firm but polite. If you find that your child's teacher is not respectful of your wishes or is downright opposed to them, you must reach some sort of agreement before you leave your child in his care. You don't want to find out later that the teacher purposely gave your child something non-vegan. Find out exactly what the teacher is opposed to so you can work on pertinent issues. Perhaps he feels it will be too much work for him to watch out for your child. That's why you need to make it as easy on him as possible. Maybe he thinks a vegan diet is unhealthy for a child. In that case you can bring in books or information for him to read. Whatever the reason, you have to make it clear that your needs must be met. If necessary, involve the principal. If the principal is opposed to veganism too, then you may have to go to the superintendent of the School Board, and so on until you can be reasonably certain that your child will not be discriminated against. Chances are that it won't come to this, but be prepared just in case.

The School Cafeteria
More than likely you'll be sending your child to school with a sack lunch. School cafeterias usually cannot accommodate vegan children in any but the barest capacities, and it doesn't look like this is going to change any time soon.

U.S. Department of Agriculture regulations require schools to serve cow's milk with each lunch in order to qualify for reimbursement of that meal. Schools that want to serve soymilk often cannot since they rely on the federal money for their program. If your child brings a note from a doctor stating that he is lactose intolerant or allergic to dairy products, some schools will be reimbursed by serving your child soymilk or calcium fortified orange juice.

Although vegans will find little to eat in school cafeterias, vegetarians are making progress. In some schools, vegetarian meals are provided for people who have religious objections to eating meat. Some schools offer a vegetarian substitution routinely, while others will offer a vegetarian option if requested. Salad bars, popular among teens, are often available in cafeterias as well. So while finding a vegan option may be next to impossible, it is gratifying to see a shift toward putting vegetarian options on the menu.

How will we get vegan options offered routinely in the school cafeteria? Three things must happen:

1. **Legislation**. As of this writing, only one U.S. state successfully passed a resolution that will put vegetarian meal options on the menus in their schools. The Hawaii State Dept. of Health, Agriculture, and Education, and the Hawaii

School Food Service passed *Senate Concurrent Resolution* (SCR151) which will "develop nutritionally sound menu plans that will provide optional vegetarian school lunches." It's a major step in the right direction. Groups in other states are attempting to pass similar resolutions. Get involved with those groups and lend them your support.

2. **Cheaper vegan foods**. It costs schools almost three times as much money to put a veggie burger on a bun than to serve a beef hamburger, mainly because the beef industry is government subsidized. Until vegan options are less expensive, or subsidized like meat and dairy products are, what choice do schools have with their limited budgets?

3. **Critical mass**. Eventually, as more children become vegetarian and vegan, and more parents demand plant-based food options, schools will have no choice but to respond to the demand. Even if you send your child to school with a packed lunch every day, be sure the school knows that you'd support a vegan option in the cafeteria. If no one speaks up, the school may assume there is no demand.

Real Stories from Real Parents:
In our school district, the grade schoolers have a vegan alternative in the form of a peanut butter sandwich. It's there every day. It's also the same thing they offer to kids who forgot their lunch money. – Rebecca

---

What's For Lunch?
If your school cafeteria is not an option, you'll be packing a vegan lunch for your child every day, along with some snacks for the break. Here are some ideas for foods that you can send in your child's lunch. Note that some of these items require a cold pack or a thermos; don't pack perishable foods unless you know they will be kept at the correct temperature.

Sandwiches. Peanut butter and jelly; veggie deli sandwich (bologna, ham, or turkey flavors) with vegan mayonnaise, mustard, and lettuce; chickpea salad in a pita pocket; mock "chicken" salad; falafel in a pita with hummus and veggies; club sandwich with avocado, veggie bacon bits, lettuce, tomato, and vegan mayonnaise.

Soup. Get out your thermos and send them with hot soup: tomato, vegetable, navy bean, minestrone or split pea! Or some vegan chili!

Salad. Garden salads with tomato, carrots, and cucumber; Chinese "chicken" salad with sweet and sour dressing; Caesar salad with vegan Caesar dressing; mock "tuna" or "egg" salad.

Veggies. Carrot, celery, or cucumber sticks; potato salad; stir-fried veggies; corn; steamed vegetables.

Leftovers from dinner. Leftovers taste great the next day, and can often be eaten cold or put into a thermos to keep them warm. For example, stews, baked potatoes, sweet potatoes, pot stickers, pizza, bean burritos, or lasagna.

Fruit. Fruit travels well. Besides the common apples, oranges, and bananas, try sending grapes, mangoes, pears, cherries, or berries.

Snacks and desserts. If you don't object to your child eating "junk" food occasionally, there are plenty of foods that you can send that are still a great deal healthier than their non-vegan versions. Cookies, donuts, candy, potato chips, pastries, and cake, to name a few. You can either make them from scratch or buy them from the store or online.

Drinks. Juice boxes, soymilk mini boxes, or water. Stay away from sodas, as even the natural sodas are packed with immune-system weakening sugar.

Sharing Lunches

How do you prevent your child from swapping his food with someone else's? How do you keep other toddlers from innocently offering your child a bite of their cheese crackers?

Preschoolers are monitored by their teachers during lunch and snack times, so you won't have to worry too much. Teachers generally instruct their students not to share lunches because someone in the group may have a severe food allergy.

If your child is in a middle grade, his lunch time activities won't be monitored as closely so he might be tempted to trade his fruit leather for someone's chocolate bar. But will he? Make sure your vegan child knows that swapping isn't safe. Be sure you're sending him with foods he really likes, so he'll be less likely to swap. Let him help select the foods he'll bring for lunch.

Older children, like those in junior high or high school, will be able to tell if an item is vegan or not by reading the label. Be sure your child knows about hidden animal ingredients.

Bullies, Teasing, and Being Different

Many parents contact me asking if their child will be teased at school for being vegan. They're worried that their children will be ostracized or beat up for being different. They wonder if they should instruct their children to lie and say they have a milk allergy rather than reveal that they are vegans. No parent wants to find out that her child is sitting all alone at lunch with no friends, or that her child is regularly ridiculed or teased for being different. So what can you do to help your child avoid being teased, bullied, or ridiculed? And how can you ensure that he won't feel "different" just for being vegan?

Don't brand your child. Sending your ten-year-old to school with a lunch of fried tofu, rice cakes, and wheat-bran cookies is sure to get him noticed. Instead, try to approximate what the other kids are eating. If you send him with peanut butter and jelly sandwiches, low fat baked potato chips, an apple, and vegan chocolate chip cookies, the other kids may not even realize that his lunch is vegan. As your child gets older, he'll be more comfortable bringing different foods to school.

There's safety in numbers. Your child is less likely to be bullied and teased if he has friends. If your child does not make friends easily, help him out a little. Invite some kids over to play, throw a party and invite his classmates, get friendly with other moms (vegan or not), and if at all possible, try to find out if there are other vegetarian kids in his class or in his grade. Having another vegan or vegetarian friend will prevent your child from feeling that he's all alone.

Teach your child how to protect herself. Martial arts classes are great for teaching self-confidence to younger and older children. Not only will your child be physically capable of defending herself, she will have less fear of being attacked. This confidence, in and of itself, may keep bullies away from her in the first place.

Teach your child verbal self-defense and the art of situation avoidance. If your child is being verbally teased, teach him how to resolve conflict with humor, role playing, creative problem solving, and cleverness. Practice handling several situations. When your child feels he has a plan, he won't be so anxious about an encounter.

Get the school involved. If your child is the victim of a bully, it is appropriate to notify school officials. Teachers are in the best position to handle bullies and keep them in check. It's possible that the school has a policy in place to handle these situations. See if they do and get their help.

Do not contact the bully's parents. Though it may be tempting to contact the parents of the kid who is bullying your child, it's often not a good idea. They may feel as if you are blaming them and get defensive. It's better to talk on neutral ground. Ask your child's teacher to host a meeting between both families to talk things out.

Instill a sense of pride in your child. It's hard to be teased about something you're proud of. Imagine if someone teased you because your hair was so darn healthy, or your grades were just too good. Let your child know often how proud you are that she is a vegan and what a tremendous gift she is giving to the planet, animals, and her own health. Speak proudly about your veganism when you're around others, too!

Real Stories from Real Parents:
If I had any advice to give to parents whose kids are being teased by their peers, it would be to concentrate on helping their children to feel happy and confident about their diet, to feel good about the part they're playing to help end the suffering of so many animals. You can explain to your children that playmates who tease them don't know what they know about food animal production, so they don't understand why it's wrong to eat animals. – Martha

---

Be aware. Be aware that not all children tell their parents when they are being bullied or teased. Some are too embarrassed or ashamed to reveal it to anyone. Look for signs that all is not well with your child. He might be afraid to walk home or take the bus, and might ask you to drive him to and from school. He may become withdrawn, distressed, or anxious. Look to see if his clothing is torn or his property destroyed. If he asks for extra money, it might be to pay someone off. Or he may cry himself to sleep at night. If you notice any of these behaviors, try to gently steer your conversations toward discussion of the behavior you're noticing, and find out if he is being victimized in any way. Then take appropriate steps as outlined above.

Field Trips
One day your child may come home from school with a field trip slip for you to sign, giving permission for him to get on a

bus and go somewhere with his class for an educational outing. No problem, in and of itself, but what if his class is taking a field trip to the zoo? Or the aquarium? Or a fast food restaurant?

Before deciding whether your child will be going on the field trip, there is a lot to consider. If your child is very young, you will make the decision for him, but as your child gets older, you should let him have more say in the matter. Following are the issues that need to be addressed.

Do you oppose patronizing these places in general? If you won't step foot inside a zoo, aquarium, or fast food restaurant, you're going to be uncomfortable allowing your child to go on a field trip to one of these places, especially without you there as a guide. What if the teacher enthusiastically applauds or endorses something you would not? If this is how you feel, explain to your child why you oppose such places and see if he will agree not to go.

Will remaining behind ostracize your child? Before handing down an executive order and forbidding your child from going, it's important to know how she feels about it. Her feelings matter. If she is very worried about being teased, ostracized, or picked on, you must weigh that into your decision. She has to know that her feelings matter to you. Remember that going to these places one time is not a sign that she's giving up her vegan ideals. Be clear with her about why you oppose such places and see if she comes home from the field trip with a similar perspective.

Call the teacher and express your concerns. A phone call to the teacher will give you a chance to explain why you oppose such places (do it gently!). Perhaps the teacher will agree with you and change the venue for the field trip. At the very least, it can't hurt to ask. Even if it's too late to change the venue this time, the teacher may be more careful in selecting a field trip location next time. This would be a good time to discuss future field trips before they are set in stone.

Look for a win/win solution. Find out what the teacher hopes to teach the students, and see if you can come up with an alternate way to accomplish the same goal. For example, if the goal of going to a zoo is to see live animals, suggest an animal rescue instead. If the goal of going to a fast food restaurant is to see how a business is run behind the scenes, suggest a vegetarian restaurant. If you can satisfy the teacher's objectives and yours at the same time, then everyone will be happy.

Let your child decide for herself. The older your children get, the more you should let them decide how they will live, and by what values. Don't assume that just because your child decides to go the zoo that she has given up her vegan values. For all you know, while she's at the zoo she could be educating her classmates on the cruel living conditions these animals endure. She might also note problems with how the animals are treated and bring them to the attention of the proper authorities.

Fundraisers

Schools use fundraisers to raise money for a variety of needs such as new programs, band uniforms, overnight field trips, and replacing worn out gym equipment. Remember your school fundraisers? What did you sell? Candy bars? Cookies? Magazine subscriptions? What if your child is asked to partake in a fundraiser where he will be selling something non-vegan? What are your options?

Opt out. If you *and* your child are opposed to the product being sold in the fundraiser, just tell your child not to participate. If you want to contribute money to the school on your child's behalf, do it without buying the product. Donate directly the amount that would have gone to the school via the product sold.

Get vegan companies involved. Contact non-profit animal rights organizations such as PETA, EarthSave, or the Farm Sanctuary and see if they have fundraising programs for schools. Also contact commercial vegan businesses and see if they have a program in place to sell their products and share profits with schools. Gather your materials and present them to the fundraising chairperson. Ask if they would consider a fundraiser with one or more of those companies next time.

Ask the school to abstain in the future. By the time you find out that your child's school is selling non-vegan candy bars, it will be too late to stop the fundraiser since contracts will have been signed. However, don't let that stop you from talking to the fundraising chairperson about why you oppose selling products from companies that directly or indirectly harm animals. Always be respectful, considerate, and polite as it's the only way you will have any effect.

To protest or not to protest? Some people might suggest protesting the fundraiser by actively asking other kids not to sell the items or even picketing the school. I don't recommend this tactic for two reasons. First, you will cause trouble for your child at school with the other children; why stir up a hornet's nest that your child has to deal with alone at school all day? Second, school officials will probably become defensive, close their ears and minds, and you will likely accomplish nothing. Protest by offering alternatives that are just as appealing – if not healthier – to everyone so it's a win-win situation.

School Parties

While I was a substitute teacher, a mother of one of my students unexpectedly popped into class 15 minutes before lunchtime. She was holding two pink boxes filled with cupcakes that she wanted to pass around to the class in honor of her son's birthday. I told her to set up her cupcakes by the door and the students could take one on their way to lunch. After the children were gone the mother offered me one of the remaining cupcakes, but I declined, telling her that I was vegan. Then I wondered what would happen if my child was a student in this class. Would she take a cupcake? Would she be able to tell that they were not vegan just by looking? Would she ask the mother questions about ingredients? What would she do if everyone were eating those items in front of her? How can you ensure that your children don't inadvertently eat non-vegan treats that find their way into their classrooms?

The answer depends on your child's age, knowledge, confidence in questioning adults about ingredients, and ability to withstand taunting and teasing.

Age. Younger children may be confused when they see a cupcake. "Mom gives me cupcakes. Those look just like hers. I can eat one." The older a child gets, however, the more likely they are to realize that the cupcake is probably not vegan. Until you're sure your children can determine that an item is probably not vegan, you're going to have to rely on the teacher to run interference. Be sure to have something stored in the classroom that the teacher can give to your child in place of the non-vegan item.

Knowledge. It can be hard to tell if a cupcake is vegan just by looking at it. Teach your child as early as possible that even though a cupcake looks like the ones you make, it may contain animal ingredients. She must not eat it unless she finds out that it's vegan.

Confidence. It's probably intimidating for children to question strangers about ingredients, especially in front of the whole class. Teach your child how to ask questions in a manner that won't be offensive to the adult. Try role playing a few scenarios, and offer suggestions for how to handle the situation if the adult is unsure of the ingredients. Also ask the teacher to step in and look out for your child when it appears as if your child is about to eat something non-vegan.

Taunting and teasing. It can be incredibly hard for a vegan child to withstand taunting and teasing from other children ("Ha ha, you don't have a cupcake!"). Teach your child appropriate defenses against taunting such as ignoring, a clever comeback, distraction, changing the subject, and telling the teacher if need be. You don't want your child caving in and eating the cupcake simply because he's being teased, so give him the tools to withstand it before it becomes an issue.

Real Stories from Real Parents:
When my son started school last November I briefly explained to his teacher that he was a vegan, and she was fine with it. I was very impressed, just before Christmas, when she explained to me that she wanted to get the children in her class a small treat, and asked if I had any suggestions on something that would be suitable for Jasper. On his last day before Christmas holidays he came home really excited because she had given them each a lollipop (vegan) and a special pencil. I was so grateful that she made the effort to be sensitive to our diet, and to Jasper's feelings. At Easter the same teacher unexpectedly gave them each a non-vegan Easter Egg. She suggested to Jasper that he could give his to someone he knew who wasn't vegan, and he proudly and happily presented it to his Uncle, with no complaints or bother at all. I was so proud of him. – Sophie

---

When Accidents Happen
You can't be with your child every moment. When you send her off to school, she's completely outside of your influence. She might accidentally eat something non-vegan, or she may do it on purpose. The key to preventing mishaps is preparation. Prepare your child to resist the temptation of eating non-vegan foods. Here's how to do that.

Knowledge and education. Weave your family's vegan values into everyday life at home. Be sure she understands your reasons for being vegan. Make sure that your child knows which ingredients are vegan and which are not. Teach her which foods are likely to be OK to eat and how to be sure.

Teacher support. Make sure that the teacher clearly understands what your child can and cannot eat, and is willing to intervene on your child's behalf to ensure that she doesn't accidentally (or purposely) eat something non-vegan. Remember to make it easy on the teacher by providing vegan snacks that can be given to your child as the need arises. Also remember that your child's teacher is not obligated to do any of this for you. Don't rely on teacher intervention alone.

Open communication. Be sure that your child is comfortable telling you if she accidentally ate something she shouldn't have. If she thinks you're going to yell at her, she won't tell you about it, and then you can't do anything to correct the situation. Be loving and understanding.

Send a good lunch. If you send her to school with food she dislikes, she may be inclined to trade for foods that look better. But if she likes the foods in her lunch, the temptation to eat something else will be far less.

Show your pride. You can also let her know how proud you are of her for resisting non-vegan foods. "Oh, I bet those cupcakes looked really good. I'm so proud of you for not taking one. And I'm sure the animals are happy too!" You may even offer to buy her the vegan equivalent of the treat she passed up.

Be active in your praise. If your child is doing everything right, don't take it for granted. Praise the good behavior and you'll get more of it. Occasionally give your child some verbal praise, a pat on the back, a hug, or take her for a special treat for no other reason than the fact that you're proud of her.

Help her handle her feelings. Some children get sad, scared, or upset when they find out they have inadvertently eaten something non-vegan. Help your child deal with her feelings by reminding her that it was an accident and that the animals will understand. Tell her that she is OK and that she is not in trouble. Find out how it happened and help ensure that it won't happen again.

> **Real Stories from Real Parents:**
> *If my son accidentally eats something he shouldn't have, I just say, "Well, now we know that that wasn't vegan. Next time you see it, you'll know not to eat it." And we just cross it off our list.* – Tayler

Remember, it's not the end of the world. You may have negative feelings as well when you find out your child ate something non-vegan. Don't scold or berate your child. Just try to make sure it won't happen again. If you get mad at your child, she may not tell you the next time it happens.

Dissection

In 1987, a tenth grade student named Jenifer Graham refused to dissect a frog in her biology class. School officials told Jenifer that unless she complied and dissected that frog, she would be given an "F" in her class. She was allowed no alternative assignment. Jenifer and her parents filed suit against the school. In the end, Jenifer was awarded an "A" in her class. That suit paved the way for other students and parents to object to dissection in the classroom. In addition, the National Anti-Vivisection Society (NAVS) set up a hotline designed to provide information, counseling and support for students, parents, and teachers who object to dissection. That number is 800-922-FROG. If you find that your child's class will be dissecting animals, take steps immediately.

Suggest alternatives. Today, alternative teaching methods exist which allow students to learn animal anatomy without ever having to dissect the animal itself. These teaching aids are available in the form of CD-ROMs, software, models, videos, and anatomy charts. NAVS has a Dissection Alternatives Loan Program, which provides students, educators, and entire schools with these choices. For a list of companies that sell alternatives to dissection, see www.vegfamily.com/lists/dissection-alternatives.htm.

Introduce a Student Choice Policy. The best way to ensure that your child will not have to participate in a dissection activity is to pass a formal Student Choice Policy. The Student Choice Policy would enable a student who objects to dissection to complete an alternate assignment. This assignment would carry the same weight as doing the dissection assignment, and would ensure that the child is not penalized in any way for choosing the alternate assignment. Either the school or the entire district can adopt this policy. To see a sample presentation for passing a Student Choice Policy, go to www.vegfamily.com/vegan-teens/student-choice-policy.htm. Following are the guidelines for a sample Student Choice Policy.

Guidelines for Sample Student Choices Policy

- Alternatives to dissection must be available in all classes that use animals.
- Students may not be penalized in any way for voicing an objection to dissection, or for requesting an alternative.
- The instructor must verbally inform his or her students of their right to an alternative prior to the day the dissection will take place.
- The alternative assignment will require the same amount of time and effort as the dissection exercise.
- The instructor, not the student, is responsible for proposing the alternative assignment. Alternatives are *not* to include watching another student dissect, taking a lower grade, or dropping the class.

- The policy must be presented to students in a non-judgmental and non-coercive manner.
- The testing procedure will not require the use of dissected specimens for those who chose an alternative.
- The school administration will monitor and ensure implementation of the Student Choice Policy.
- The policy will be incorporated into existing curriculum guidelines and the student handbook.
- The policy also allows for alternatives to live animal experiments, insect collections, or any classroom activity that involves animals or their body parts. The student who requests an alternative should have the option of leaving the room while dissection is taking place.

Support your child. It can be very difficult for your child to inform his teacher that he is opposed to dissection, especially in front of his peers. Offer to help your child talk with the teacher or principal, and strive to come up with an agreeable alternative that allows your child to learn the necessary lesson without doing the dissection. Be sure to praise your child for having the courage to stand up for his beliefs.

Get support from other parents. Find other parents and students who may be opposed to the dissection and ask for their assistance in finding an alternative to dissection in the classroom. Perhaps they can help you get a Student Choice Policy passed.

Getting Involved

If people like you aren't willing to speak up for what you believe in, nothing will ever change. If you want vegan options on the school lunch menu, if you want to stop classroom dissection, or if you want teachers to stop taking kids to the zoo on field trips, then you have to be willing to step in and get involved.

When you get involved in your child's school you'll be in a better position to suggest changes and alternatives to normal procedures. Here are some suggestions and guidelines for making a difference in your child's education and at his school.

Help out in the classroom. Due to the large class sizes in many school districts, there has been a push to have parents help out in the classroom as assistants. If your school offers such a program, and you are available, volunteer to be a classroom aide. You will get a chance to see your child in a classroom environment, and see who he spends time with during breaks. You will also form a better relationship with the teacher, making it easier to talk to him about important issues later. You'll probably also find that your child enjoys having you around.

Join the PTA. When you join the local Parent-Teacher-Association you will be in a position to influence programs, gifts to the schools, and fundraising activities. The PTA also gets involved in promoting the welfare of students, so you'll be in a great position to represent the wishes and needs of vegan and vegetarian parents.

Educate students. Offer to give a vegan cooking demonstration in your child's classroom. You can bring samples of vegan products or just the empty boxes from your home. Let the students help you make vegan cookies or fruit smoothies, while you teach them about the health benefits of being vegan. Make it fun and the teacher will invite you back for more demonstrations. If you're willing, offer to do the same demonstration or talk for other classrooms.

Volunteer. If you can't volunteer to be a classroom assistant, try to volunteer for special events. Your vegan influence might make a difference. For example, if the school is having a bake sale you can send your best vegan treats – labeled as such – to be sold with the other non-vegan items. Or if they are having a carnival, you can steer them toward vegan snacks like popcorn and pretzels, instead of ice cream and candy.

Get to know school officials. Be sure to introduce yourself to the staff at your child's school and make pleasant contact often. You never know when you'll need the ear of the school principal, cafeteria manager, or other employees.

Avoid arguing with teachers, other parents, or school officials. If you find yourself in a situation where you need to take a stand on an issue, always be polite and respectful. Once a discussion turns into an argument, people will stop listening to your points. Even if you aren't able to sway people to your way of thinking, as long as you are respectful people will be open to hearing what you have to say the next time you need to bring something up.

Chapter 6

SOCIAL SITUATIONS

Aside from school, there will be other situations to challenge the vegan child. What should you do when your child attends a friend's birthday party and the hosts are not serving anything your child can eat? How do you throw a vegan birthday party for your child? Can your child go to summer camp, and will his diet be accommodated? How do you find a vegan playgroup so that your child will have vegan friends? Is there a way to easily find vegan families in your area? Can you get vegan meals at a special event such as a wedding? How will your family handle holiday meals, and will being vegan cause holidays to become a source of friction among family members?

Knowing the answers to these questions will save you time and worry. Figure out how to handle awkward social situations before they strike, not at the last minute. Your child will thank you.

Formal Catered Affairs
Your family receives an invitation to a formal, catered affair such as a wedding, bar mitzvah, or engagement party, and you know that in all probability, vegan meals won't be on

the menu. What should you do? Basically, you have three options:

- Ask the host or caterer to accommodate your special dietary needs, in advance
- Wait until you get to the party and then ask for something vegan, or eat only the items that you think are vegan
- Eat before you go so you're not hungry during the party

Ask for a vegan meal ahead of time. This works best when you and the host are close friends or relatives. When you receive your invitation, the response card may ask what sort of meal you prefer. Usually the options are chicken, fish, beef, or vegetarian. Don't just select vegetarian and hope your meal will be vegan. Likely, it will not. Write on the card that you need x number of vegan meals and send it in. A few days later call the host and discuss your dietary needs. Find out what the menu consists of, and ask the host if she can arrange with the caterer to prepare a few vegan meals for your family. If the host or caterer is unaccustomed to serving vegan guests, make some suggestions for simple meals like grilled or steamed vegetables over steamed white rice, a fruit plate, pasta with marinara sauce, a large salad, or a baked potato.

If the host seems uncomfortable asking the caterer to prepare special meals, offer to speak to the caterer directly. When caterers have enough advance notice, it's usually no problem for them to make vegan meals. In fact, your meal will probably be easier to prepare than the other meals. If you do make your arrangements directly with the caterer be sure to call three days before the event to confirm your meal choice.

If the host seems unwilling to accommodate your special request and isn't comfortable letting you speak with the caterer, stop there. Remember, it's just one meal. There's no need to ruin a friendship or create family friction over one meal. The focus, after all, is the event itself.

Wait until you get there. If you don't know the host well or you don't feel comfortable asking for a special meal, wait until you get to the party to see if you can find something vegan to eat. You could also ask the catering staff to make you an impromptu vegan meal.

Appetizers are served at many formal events, and you can usually find fruit or raw vegetables. Load up on those before you sit down to the meal. If you're lucky, the salad will have an Italian dressing and will probably be vegan (but be sure to ask the server what ingredients are in the dressing). If you ordered the vegetarian plate thinking you might get something vegan by chance, you may be looking at lasagna with cheese. It may be better to ask what comes with the meat meal because the side dishes are often vegan; for example, a baked potato, rice pilaf, green beans or other vegetables. Make sure these items are vegan before you eat them, and ask them to leave the meat off your plate.

An alternative to winging it is to locate the catering staff when you first arrive at the event. Tell them about your dietary needs, and see if they can put something together for you. At my husband's high school reunion we were able to get a plate of spaghetti with marinara sauce. At my aunt and uncle's anniversary party we had a plate of grilled veggies over rice with a baked potato, a large salad, and some sourdough rolls – by just asking when we got to the event. Be very clear with the staff about what you cannot eat (milk, butter, eggs, cheese, etc.) and offer suggestions for what you can eat (vegetables, potatoes, rice, salad, etc.) Whatever you do, don't ask for something complicated. Keep it simple.

Eat before you go. The prudent thing to do in any case is to eat a little something before you go. Even if you've been assured that a vegan meal is waiting for you, it's wise to be wary. Be sure to feed your toddlers and kids ahead of time too, just in case the meal doesn't appeal to them or you end up with just fruit. Another idea is to put some energy bars or nuts in your car or purse so that you can slip away unnoticed for a quick snack if necessary.

We were at a kosher wedding once where we'd arranged with the hostess to have a vegan meal ahead of time. The only problem was that when she explained our needs to the caterer she said we didn't eat meat or dairy products. So when we arrived we discovered that everything on our plate had eggs in it, which, according to kosher law, is not dairy. Luckily, we had eaten before going to that wedding so we were not hungry during the reception.

Informal Parties and Gatherings
What if the party your family has been invited to is informal, such as an outdoor barbecue, potluck, or celebration? What is appropriate in these situations? Here are some tips for eating vegan at informal events.

Outdoor barbecues. Barbecues are easy because even if the host is not serving anything vegan, it should be no problem to bring some of your own food. You can bring veggie burgers, tofu dogs, vegetable skewers, or corn on the cob, and use their barbecue to cook it. Try to get your food cooked on a different part of the grill than where the meat is cooking, or ask if you can cook your food first. You can also wrap your food in tin foil so it touches neither the grill nor meat. If you don't want your food cooked on the same grill, bring other dishes like vegan potato salad, coleslaw, baked beans, potato chips, or salad. Or ask if you can use the microwave or oven to heat your veggie burger. You'll probably be able to use their condiments and fixings (ketchup, mustard, relish, lettuce, tomato, and onion), but you may have to bring your own buns.

Potlucks. If you're attending a potluck where your family will be the only vegans, you should bring more than one dish; you may be eating only the food you brought. Bring a casserole, salad, fruit, and a dessert for yourselves. If you're very lucky, someone will bring a dish that happens to be vegan, but don't count on it. Bring more than enough for just your family so other people can sample your vegan fare.

If you're in a position to request that other people bring vegan items, do it. Some people might be more than willing to accommodate you; in fact, they might even enjoy the challenge.

Real Stories from Real Parents:
Our office was having a potluck the day before Thanksgiving. The person in charge of coordinating the event asked a few people if they would bring vegan dishes. Only one person was unwilling to accommodate this request. Other people came up to me and asked me about ingredients and seemed very eager to try making something new. The potluck turned out really well and everyone enjoyed their dishes. – Patricia

---

Celebrations. Celebrations can include graduation parties, religious ceremonies, homecoming parties, house warming parties, and the like. They often take place in someone's home or backyard, with the host providing all the food. In this case, contact the hostess and find out what she is planning to serve. Mention that your family is vegan and ask if it would be OK to bring some of your own food. Reassure the hostess that you will be no extra trouble.

Sometimes the hostess will offer to make foods that are vegan in deference to you. In that case it's all right to mention some things you can eat that will also appeal to the rest of her guests, or you might offer to send her some of your recipes if she is doing a lot of cooking. The only problem with this approach is that she may accidentally make something non-vegan because of her inexperience with hidden ingredients. It would be rude of you to question her about all the food she's made if she already assured you that it would be vegan. If you are not completely certain that the host can make vegan food for you, you're better off bringing your own food.

> **Real Stories from Real Parents:**
> *On one occasion one of my family members went out of his way to buy some vegan desserts for a gathering we were having. These items definitely didn't look vegan but he insisted that the bakery said there was no dairy in them. He also seemed a little miffed that his act of kindness was being met with such suspicion. So, I ate the baked goods. Later we found out that all the items had eggs in them. Instead of being apologetic, my relative complained that it was too hard to buy food for us, and since then we've almost always had to bring our own food to these events.* – Gillian

Birthday Parties

Ah, the birthday party. Nothing worries a grandmother more than thinking of her vegan grandchild sitting alone in a corner at a schoolmate's birthday party with nothing to eat and no one to play with. I get more questions about birthday parties than any other event. Your child will go to a lot of birthday parties while growing up, and it's possible that none of them will be vegan except his own. That's OK. With a little preparation and planning, your child will have fun at every birthday party, including his own.

Birthday party at a friend's house. If your child is attending a party at his friend's house, call the host to find out what food is being served. If there's nothing vegan on the menu, tell the host that you'd like to send along some food for your child, and ask if she can please give it to your child when the other kids start eating. Reassure the host that the food you're sending will be easy to prepare. Try to send similar foods. For example if they are having hot dogs, send tofu dogs. If they are having pizza, send cheeseless pizza or pizza with vegan cheese.

Also find out what they'll be having for dessert and send the vegan equivalent. Cupcakes are easy to transport and you can send extra for other kids who may be on restrictive diets. You can send a quart of your child's favorite vegan ice cream and offer to let the host keep the leftovers.

Real Stories from Real Parents:
My 10-year-old son takes a little more than his share of vegan treats to birthday parties so that he can have lots of "junk" to eat. His friends often have pizza parties, so I send him with an Amy's non-dairy pizza that I've doctored up. – Misty

---

Birthday party at a specialized party place. Sometimes parents hold birthday parties at party places such as arcades, ice skating rinks, miniature golf courses, kids' gyms, carnivals, etc. There may be no facilities to prepare, assemble, or heat up food. In this case, send your child with a backpack full of non-perishable vegan foods. That way if there's nothing else he can eat, at least he won't go hungry. It's wise to feed your child before this type of event.

Birthday party at a fast food restaurant. Sometimes parties are held in fast food restaurants like McDonald's. If you know there is nothing on the menu that your child can eat, you'll have to prepare an alternative. At some fast food restaurants your child will be able to eat the french fries or salad (as long as you send some dressing to go with it). But you can't always count on this as an option, as many contain animal-based flavorings.

Slumber parties. Older kids, especially girls, like to have slumber parties. In this case you should definitely send along food and snacks, since your child will be there overnight. Also, find out what the host is serving for breakfast and send an equivalent such as cereal with a container of soymilk, frozen waffles, veggie sausages, or pre-cooked tofu scramble that can be easily reheated.

Your child's birthday party. A lot of parents wonder if they should serve non-vegan food at their kid's birthday party to accommodate guests who are not vegan. It's entirely your choice. My advice is to plan to make the party entirely vegan. If someone complains, so what? What's the worst that can happen? If they're overly concerned about not having meat or dairy products at your party, suggest they eat before they come. Do not encourage people to bring animal products into your home if you don't want them to. You may be pleasantly surprised, as I have been, that people enjoy vegan food so much that they forget they are eating something without animal products.

At the last brunch I hosted, I served bagels with vegan cream cheese, Chinese chicken salad (minus the chicken), chips and guacamole, raw vegetables with hummus, fruit salad, vegan potato salad, rolls with margarine, and cashews. For dessert we had chocolate cake and lemon coconut cake (purchased from a local vegan baker) with four kinds of vegan ice cream. Our guests remarked on how wonderful everything tasted, and everyone forgot they were eating vegan food.

Summer Camps

Remember going to summer camp when you were a kid? Hanging out with friends, swimming, canoeing, telling ghost stories at night, hiking and – oh yes – the food! Do vegan parents send their kids to summer camp? Are there vegan summer camps? What should you do if all of your kids' friends are going to camp and your child wants to go too, but the camp doesn't serve vegan meals? Can she still go?

Vegan summer camps. Yes, there are vegan summer camps for kids (and adults), but you may be spending a lot of money on airfare since chances are they won't be anywhere near where you live. There are only a handful of truly vegan summer camps on Earth.

One advantage of sending your child to an all-vegan summer camp is that you'll know she'll be fed properly. She'll also meet other vegan children her age, so she will know that she's not alone. The disadvantages are the airfare and the fact that probably none of her non-vegan friends will go with her. If she wants to meet other vegan kids, though, then sending her to a vegan summer camp is the way to go!

There are also camps you can go to as a family, which is a great way to meet other families and talk about raising vegan kids.

To find a vegan summer camp, do a search online and see if you can find one in your country. Contact Vegetarian groups or animal rights organizations in your area to see if they have a recommendation.

Vegetarian summer camps. Yes, there are vegetarian summer camps, and there are a lot more of them than vegan camps. You might be able to find a vegetarian camp within a 300-mile radius of your home. The staff is more likely to accommodate vegan meals than a regular summer camp. So if you need to compromise, try one of these.

Regular summer camps. If your child wants to go to the same summer camp as his non-vegan friends, don't discourage it. He needs to know that being vegan doesn't preclude him from participating in fun events. Call the director of the camp and tell him that your son is vegan and would like to attend the camp. Ask him how they handle dietary restrictions. If they have no policy in place, start making suggestions. You have three options: the camp supplies your child with vegan meals, you supply the camp with some alternatives they can serve your child, or you send your child with enough food to last him the entire time he's at camp.

If the camp is willing to supply meals for your child, make sure they know what they're doing. You don't want to find out later that they fed your child honey, whey or casein. Ask to sit down with them and go over exactly what they plan to serve. Make suggestions and give them a list of foods and ingredients your child can and cannot eat. Be sure to thank them for being accommodating by sending a thank you note to the director and food manager after camp is over, and maybe just prior, which serves as a good reminder.

If the camp is unwilling or incapable of providing special meals for your child, ask if you can do the shopping and drop off food for your child at the camp. We're not talking about anything complicated. Think frozen dinners, cans of chili or soup, peanut butter and jelly with vegan bread, veggie deli slices, spaghetti with marinara, fresh fruit and vegetables, but nothing that takes a long time to prepare. Make sure the staff is willing to at least prepare the food you send. The camp may even deduct the cost of meals if you provide your own.

In the rare case that the staff won't provide or even prepare anything for your child, then the only way your child is going to this camp is if you pack up a suitcase full of non-perishable foods that he can eat when there's nothing vegan on the table. Most likely, he'll be able to get fresh fruit and vegetables while at camp, but that won't sustain him for long. Some ideas for things to pack include: energy bars, serving-sized soymilk boxes and cereals, bread, a jar of peanut butter, applesauce, trail mix, dried fruit, nuts, granola, bagels, cookies and other treats, popcorn, pretzels, and juice boxes. As you can see from this list, his nutrition is going to suffer a bit while at camp, but he won't starve.

The bottom line is that if there's a will, there's a way. If your child really wants to go, find a way to get him there. Camp is a great experience for kids, vegan or not.

Girl Scouts and Boy Scouts

Scouting can be such a wonderful experience. Both my husband and I have fond memories of our experience as scouts. My husband spent a lot of time camping and getting merit badges. He learned how to survive in the wilderness, treat snakebite, and save someone who was drowning. As a Girl Scout, I had fun selling cookies, learning how to cross-stitch, and telling ghost stories by the campfire. Looking back, we both feel that we got a lot out of it, and hope our daughter will someday become a Girl Scout. Can vegans be scouts? Absolutely. Here are some areas of concern and advice for dealing with them.

Selling Girl Scout cookies. Most of the Girl Scout cookies I sold went right into our own freezer. My mom was very willing to support "the cause." But Girl Scout cookies are far from vegan, and you may not want your daughter selling them. What should you do?

One idea is to simply have her opt out. Selling cookies is not mandatory. At least then you won't be directly supporting a non-vegan practice.

Another option is to purchase some of the cookies and donate them to a homeless shelter. In this way the cookies are being used to feed homeless people, and you're supporting your daughter's troop.

A third option is not to buy any cookies, but instead make a donation directly to your daughter's troop. It can be for the amount they would have received if you had bought a few boxes of cookies.

A fourth option is to contact a vegan cookie company and see if you can sell their cookies instead of the official Girl Scout cookies. Donate the proceeds to your daughter's troop.

A fifth option is to try to get the entire troop *not* to sell cookies, but to have another type of fundraiser instead. If you're lucky, everyone in the troop will agree with your reasons and see it as an opportunity to really do some good. But it's a long shot.

Pancake breakfasts. In my husband's Boy Scout troop, they held pancake breakfasts. Each scout sold tickets to people in the neighborhood, and the scouts would prepare pancakes and sausages for everyone who showed up. If your son's troop is going to have a pancake breakfast, here are some options for handling the situation.

First, he can opt out and simply choose not to participate. Second, he can participate and simply not eat any of the pancakes or sausages. Instead of cooking the items, he can take tickets, pour juice, or help clean up. Third, you can make a donation in his name to the troop and not attend the breakfast. Fourth, you can buy some tickets and give them to homeless people so they can eat breakfast. Fifth, you can offer to make vegan pancakes and sausages for people who want them, although this will probably not be the best use of your time and energy.

Snack time. I'm not sure how most troops handle snack time during a meeting, but in my troop, each mom was responsible for providing a snack to all the girls in the troop on a rotating basis. Some moms baked cookies or made popcorn balls, while other moms served cookies or pastries from the store. How should you handle this?

When it's your turn to provide the snack make sure you serve something really great so the kids know that vegan snacks and treats are delicious. You don't want to be the only mom serving carrot sticks when all the other moms are sending donuts and cakes. When someone else is providing the snack, be sure to send your daughter with something she can eat in case the snack is not vegan. You may also want to make a list of some healthy, vegan snacks that other moms can find and serve to the troop.

Camping. Camping is great fun for both boys and girls. If your child has the opportunity to go camping with his troop, let him. All you have to do is make sure he'll have plenty to eat on the trip.

First get a sense of the Scoutmaster's maturity level. If he's a young person himself (say 22 to 26) he may not care what your child eats. Older Scoutmasters (say 26 to 40) will probably be able to handle making sure your child isn't teased, his food isn't hidden by the other kids, and that he gets enough to eat. If the Scoutmaster is over 40, he may not even agree with you that being vegan is healthy and may see camping as an opportunity to feed your child meat or dairy products. If you think the Scoutmaster will not enforce your wishes, you may not want to let your child go on the camping trip. These are generalizations, and ultimately you will have to decide how your Scoutmaster will enforce your wishes.

If you think the Scoutmaster will look after your child's needs, consult with him regarding food and find out what he's planning to bring. Look at the list, see what's vegan, make suggestions for vegan versions of items he's planning to serve, and add some ideas of your own.

For example, if the Scoutmaster is bringing potato chips, tell him which brands your child can eat so he can get those for everyone. If he's serving hot dogs and hamburgers, see if he'll buy some vegan versions for your child and anyone else who wants them, *and* make sure that the buns will be vegan. If they're going to have cereal for breakfast, let him know which cereals your child can eat. Make sure there will be soymilk to go with it.

Send emergency snacks like energy bars, trail mix, dried fruit, juice boxes, and desserts so your child will have enough to eat when the rest of the troop is eating mostly non-vegan foods.

If the Scoutmaster wants other parents along to help out, go! Then you can then easily make sure your child's needs are taken care of.

Field trips. Our troop leaders took us on field trips to McDonald's, the police station, and a flower shop, so we could see what it was like behind the scenes. I'll admit that it was great fun seeing how a McDonald's works, because at the time I was one of their best customers! If your child's troop is going on a field trip to a non-vegan location, try to suggest an alternative. If you can't get the venue changed to something neutral (like a flower shop or police station), then you'll have to make the best of the situation. If the plan is to go to a fast food restaurant, find out if they plan to eat there. If so, you can pick up your child early, before the other kids sit down to eat, or if there is something vegan on the menu, let her eat that. Alternatively, you could send her with a packed lunch.

Be the leader. What would happen if *you* were the leader of your child's troop? Think of the opportunities that you'd have to educate and inspire other children to live cruelty-free. For example, you could select the field trip locations such as an animal rescue or vegan restaurant. You could bring only vegan food on the camping trips. You could possibly convince the kids not to sell Girl Scout cookies at all, but instead have some other fundraiser, such as selling crafts, selling services (like running errands for busy parents or the elderly), or selling tickets to a play put on by the troop. You could bring in guest speakers to your meetings who might do vegan cooking demonstrations or talk about animal rights. Be careful not to turn the troop into a pulpit for vegan preaching, otherwise the other parents will pull their kids out, and then you'll have accomplished nothing. Just find simple ways to incorporate cruelty-free living into the scouting experience.

Camping Trips

Speaking of camping trips, here are some great tips for what to eat when you go camping. If you've got a gas stove, all the better.

Breakfast. Cereal with soymilk, tofu scramble, sautéed potatoes, pancakes, veggie bacon, veggie sausage patties.

Lunch. Sandwiches, potato chips, fruit salad, potato salad, garden salad.

Dinner. Veggie burgers and tofu dogs, spaghetti with marinara sauce, garlic bread, stir-fried veggies, baked beans, canned foods.

Snacks. Trail mix, nuts, dried fruit, vegan jerky, fruit bars, energy bars, rice cakes.

Desserts. Cookies, pudding, chocolate bars, donuts, candy.

Finding Other Vegan Families

It's wonderful to have other vegan families in your life. It's easier to have picnics, potlucks, birthday parties, and play dates. You never have to ask, "Is there cheese in that casserole you made?" And it's nice to be around people who understand who you are and what you're about. But how do you find vegan families in your area? It's not like we put a big "V" on the door signifying our chosen lifestyle.

Considering that vegans make up such a small part of the population, the odds are against finding more than a few vegan families in any one city. Of course, some cities have larger populations of vegans than others. But don't be discouraged. Here are some ideas for finding other vegan families in your neighborhood.

Check the health food stores. If you're buying vegan items in a health food store, chances are that there are other vegans buying the same items or the store wouldn't bother to stock them. Observe whether the health food store has a community bulletin board. If it does, post a flyer that says, "Vegan family looking to connect with other vegan families in this area. If interested, please call (list phone number)." Also, look to see if other families have already posted a similar flyer, and call them.

While shopping, see if you can spot other vegans by what they have in their carts. If you see a parent with a three-year-old in tow who's putting all vegan items in the cart, strike up a conversation. Talk about food, ask if she's vegan, and mention that you're vegan too. Who knows, you may end up exchanging phone numbers.

Look for potlucks. Check the community bulletin board for vegan potlucks in your area. Potlucks are a great way to meet and interact with people before committing to becoming friends. Also, go to *vegetarian* potlucks, because lots of vegans attend those as well.

Join organizations. Contact national organizations and find out whether they have local chapters in your area. If they don't, start one. Try EarthSave, the Vegan Society, and the Vegetarian Society. These organizations often have events, meetings, dinners, fundraisers, and potlucks. You're sure to meet other like-minded families at these events.

Volunteer at events. If there are any environmental, vegetarian, animal rights, or vegan events in your area, volunteer to help out. Working with others on a good cause is a fast way to find new friends.

Real Stories from Real Parents:
I volunteered to monitor the children's area at a vegan festival. By the end of the day I had the phone numbers of three other vegan moms, and now my son has several new vegan playmates. – Josie

---

Check the Internet. Go online and find vegan message boards. Then post a message asking if there are any vegan families in your neighborhood. Do not give out personal information online, such as your address or phone number. If you do decide to meet someone, meet in a public place until you're certain it's safe to get more personal.

Frequent vegan restaurants. If you're lucky enough to have a vegan restaurant in your area, ask the manager if they ever host vegan meetings, gatherings, or fundraisers. Or look around for other families dining there and casually strike up a conversation on your way out. Obviously you don't want to pester people, but there's nothing wrong with some light banter. They may be looking for vegan families, too.

Forming Playgroups

Now that you've found other vegan families in your area, consider forming a playgroup. Playgroups are great fun for kids and parents. The benefits of being part of a playgroup include having other parents to discuss challenges with, fostering friendships between the children, going on trips and excursions together, and sharing recipes, stories, and ideas for raising vegan children.

Following are some ideas for finding or forming a vegan playgroup and how to keep it running smoothly.

Find out if a playgroup already exists in your area. If you've hooked up with other vegan families, ask the parents if they know of any vegan playgroups in your area. If they don't know of any, consult with the local chapters of national organizations such as EarthSave to find out if they have a vegan families group. You can also go online to www.vegfamily.com/playgroups/index.htm where you will find a current list of veg-friendly playgroups.

If you can't find one, form one. It has to start somewhere, right? Don't be shy about starting your own vegan playgroup. The worst case scenario is that no one joins, and you've lost nothing but a little time. In the best case, you end up with a thriving vegan playgroup. You can make it as much or as little work as you're willing to put into it. And once people join, you can offload some of the administrative details to other volunteers.

Decide on an age group. Some playgroups limit ages of the kids to less than five years old, while others range from birth to twelve. If you select a wide range, be prepared to provide a variety of activities for the older children while keeping the limitations of young toddlers in mind.

Decide how often you will meet. Some playgroups meet weekly; others meet once a month. You can start off meeting once per month and then go weekly if that's what everyone wants to do.

Real Stories from Real Parents:
Our playgroup started out meeting weekly. We started with 12 families. But over time the group dwindled to just four families. We decided to just meet once a month and our attendance soared to 16 families! My kids have a ball at these big, potluck events. We never miss it! – Vicki

---

Pick a specific day and time. It's probably best for scheduling if you pick a set day each week or month (i.e., every Friday or the first Saturday of the month). That way people who can come to one meeting will probably be able to come every time. If you move the day around too much you'll gain some families but lose others. If you select a weekday, you'll probably get more moms than dads. If you select a weekend, you'll get more dads involved, but may get fewer families, since weekends are often filled with other activities.

Time is an important consideration, too. If you meet in the morning, you will get toddlers and babies and perhaps some of the older home schooled children. If you want to include kids who go to school, you'll probably have to meet after 3 pm.

Set food guidelines. Be clear with all members about what food is allowed at the meetings. If you're having a potluck, it's probably best to ask people to bring only vegan items so that everyone can eat them. If you have vegetarians in the group, decide if you're comfortable having them bring non-vegan food just for their kids or if you want them to only bring vegan food to the meetings. Make a handout with your food policy on it and give it to new members when they join the group.

Real Stories from Real Parents:
Our playgroup has a strict policy about food. Everything has to be vegan. The vegetarians don't seem to mind, although one time someone brought what they thought was vegan cheese, but it had casein in it. Once we pointed it out to her she was so mortified. Luckily, none of the kids had a chance to eat it before we got rid of it. – Rebecca

---

Pick a meeting place for the playgroup. You can host the gathering at your house, but be sure that your house is baby-proofed and that you are comfortable having lots of people in your home. Or you can rotate the meetings at all members' houses. Many playgroups meet at parks, museums, play places, or recreation rooms.

Advertise your playgroup. Use word of mouth, flyers posted at health food stores, and announcements at vegetarian and vegan events to attract members to your playgroup. List a phone number or email address so that people can contact you with questions.

Have special events. Besides meeting weekly or monthly, you can organize special events such as camping trips, field trips to museums, trips to an amusement park, sleepovers, outdoor barbecues, swim parties, Halloween parties, themed potlucks, movie nights, and holiday parties. Special events are a great way to involve dads who may not otherwise be available to participate.

Invite guest speakers to your group. If your group is large enough, you may be able to get guest speakers to come to the group and give a talk or demonstration. Good choices include authors, environmental group leaders, shelter employees, vegan restaurant managers, or someone who can do a cooking demonstration.

Keeping in touch. Most people will probably have email. Use it to keep in touch with your members and to announce plans and events. Not having to call everyone will save you a lot of time.

Ask for help. Don't take on the burden of planning, preparing, and cleaning up all by yourself, especially if your group is large. Ask other members to help you plan special events, hold meetings at their homes, make phone calls, draft flyers, make announcements, table events, etc. If you get burned out, the playgroup may fall apart.

Handling the Holidays

There are two reactions I usually get when I talk to vegans about holidays. Some people have no trouble spending holidays with their families after they go vegan, while others just can't do it. For the latter, holidays can become a source of friction, especially when spent with relatives who are unsupportive of a vegan lifestyle. Often there is a dead carcass on the table that people are praying over and feasting upon. It can be very distressing to sit around a table watching family members gnaw and pull on the body parts of an innocent animal, especially as they are giving thanks for the blessings in their lives.

Should you stop going to these events? Should you insist they serve only vegan foods out of respect to you? Should you sit quietly with your vegan meal while all around you people are eating meat and dairy products? Is there a way to compromise so everyone is happy?

There are no simple answers; every family is different. You must decide for yourself how to handle this situation. You have a right to abstain from sitting at a table with people who are eating meat. On the other hand, what right do you have to expect other people to conform to your lifestyle when they don't agree with it and they are perfectly content with their own? Some people suggest compromising, while others say that to sit at a table with meat-eaters is too great a sacrifice.

You've got to find your comfort level. No one can tell you how to feel or react in this type of situation. You have many options open to you, though. See if any of the following ideas work for you.

Bring your own meal. If you're comfortable doing so, bring a separate vegan meal for your family and eat it when everyone else is eating their meal. You don't need to draw attention to yourselves and you don't need to justify what you're doing. If your extended family will view this as a snub of their food or hospitality, then make sure they know in advance why you'll be bringing a separate meal for your vegan family.

When I was a child, my grandmother used to bring a kosher meal for my grandfather and her to our Thanksgiving holiday. I never really noticed that she was eating any differently than we were, and she never brought it up or asked anyone else to eat kosher. I wonder now if it bothered her that the rest of her Jewish family was not eating kosher. There was never any mention of it, and everyone seemed to have a good time at the event.

Contribute a dish or two. How about bringing a couple of vegan dishes to share with the rest of your family? Sharing is a great way to introduce them to vegan versions of their old time favorites without forcing it on anyone. Be sure to bring plenty of food for yourself so you'll have enough to eat too.

Help with the meal preparation. If you're in the kitchen helping prepare some of the food, you might be able to make something vegan that was not originally intended to be vegan. For example, you could put balsamic vinaigrette on the salad instead of a bleu cheese dressing, or use margarine and soymilk in the mashed potatoes instead of butter and milk. Offer your recipes to the hosts and see if they want to incorporate them into the menu.

> **Real Stories from Real Parents:**
> *In my family we do potluck holiday meals so no one person has the burden of doing all the cooking. I remember one year, right after I went vegan, I told my family that I was going to bring the dessert to the Christmas dinner. When I arrived with my apple and pumpkin pies, I noticed that someone else had brought dessert too. I was so hurt that they were "covering their bases" in case they didn't like what I brought. But once they tried my pies, they were amazed! Now they ask me to bring them every year. –* Susan

Arrive before or after the meal. If you enjoy your family's company but are opposed to watching them eat meat, consider attending the event, but leaving before the meal is served or arriving after the meal is eaten. This may be a good compromise, since your children can spend time with their relatives and you can avoid the unpleasantness of watching family members eat dead animals.

Spend holidays with other vegan families. If you've decided you simply cannot be at an event where meat is being served, consider spending your holiday with other vegan families. Then you'll have the benefit of celebrating the holiday with other people, and get a vegan meal as well. You can trade off the hosting responsibilities each year, or have potlucks. If you're members of a playgroup, this might be a good event to share as well.

Spend the holidays with just your own family. If you don't want to attend your extended family's gathering and you don't know any other vegan families, you can have a celebration of your own. Make it just as festive as you would if lots of people were coming. Make an elaborate meal, decorate your home, do crafts with the kids, play games after dinner, and have a special vegan dessert. Make it a memory your children will cherish.

Host the holiday yourself. If your family is willing, why not host the holiday and invite everyone over for a vegan feast? Be sure that you pull out all the stops and make the best recipes you've got. This is not the time to experiment with recipes you haven't perfected yet. Make your tried-and-true recipes, the ones you know will come out perfectly every time and will knock their socks off! Your hope is to convince your family that a vegan meal can be both enjoyable and compassionate so that they'll want to do it again the next year.

In fact, don't wait for a holiday to invite your family over for a nice vegan meal. If you share your delicious foods with them on non-holidays, they might actually request that you bring these foods to holiday dinners.

Avoid debates and arguments. Nothing ruins a party like friction, arguing, and debates. If someone picks a fight, teases, or tries to get your child to eat meat, be the bigger person and let it roll off your back. Don't stoop to their level. Use humor to diffuse a hostile situation and deflect criticism. Don't get drawn into a heated discussion. If it's unbearable, leave gracefully.

By the same token, don't go to your family's holiday event with the sole purpose of berating people or trying to make them feel guilty about eating meat. They will close their minds, everyone will be uncomfortable, and you won't have made any difference. Don't use holiday gatherings as a pulpit. If you don't agree with what they are doing and can't refrain from commenting on it, don't go to their event.

Educate and inspire. The best way to enact change is to be an example. Go to the party with the best vegan food in your arsenal. Sit there and actively enjoy your meal, and talk about how glad you are to be among family members.

Let them ask you what you're eating and offer them a bite. Entice them with your food and easy-going demeanor. People are more open to change when they are not being attacked.

Handling disagreements with your partner. What if your partner wants to go to the family event and is content bringing his own food, but you don't want anything to do with a party where people are eating meat? Or what if your wife wants to bring a Tofurkey but you're sure your mother will be offended? There's going to have to be a compromise. Here are some options. Your partner goes to the event and you do not. Or you switch off each year, first going to the event together and the next year staying home or doing something with friends. Or you find a way that you can both be happy, such as hosting a vegan gathering. Remember, it's one day, one meal. Don't let disagreements ruin your relationship with your spouse or partner.

Easter and Halloween
There are at least two holidays that seem particularly oriented toward kids and are obviously big money makers for candy companies: Easter and Halloween. Will your vegan child be able to partake in Easter egg hunts and trick-or-treating fun? For sure! Here are some tips to make Easter and Halloween (and any other kid-friendly holiday) as fun for your kids as they were for you.

Easter baskets. My mom used to give my siblings and me an Easter basket every year, even though we were Jewish. I loved getting my Easter basket! She filled it with jellybeans, chocolate eggs, marshmallow Peeps, hollow chocolate bunnies, and sometimes toys or stuffed animals. What can you put in a vegan child's Easter basket? Plenty! Here are some ideas: vegan gummi bears, vegan jellybeans, vegan chocolate eggs, vegan donuts, and hard candies. Also, if you visit vegan chocolate companies online at Easter time, you may find some special chocolates in the shapes of eggs and bunnies. You can also put non-food items in the basket, like pencils, rulers, toys, games, stuffed animals, and books.

Easter eggs. Should vegan kids decorate Easter eggs? Decorating eggs is really not a very vegan thing to do. For one, you've got to buy eggs from the store, something you normally would not do. Then you're hard boiling the egg, and decorating it with dyes. Now you've got a pretty, but essentially useless, egg that's going to go to waste. So not only have you purchased eggs, but you're going to waste them or give them to someone to eat.

Perhaps a better idea is to let your kids decorate plastic eggs. I'm visualizing glue, glitter, buttons, fabric, rhinestones, lace, and other assorted craft items. They won't "go bad," and they harm no one. Plus, I believe they're even prettier than real eggs.

> **Real Stories from Real Parents:**
> *Our church put on an Easter day celebration for the kids. We had fun with face painting and crafts, but when my daughter saw the kids dyeing their eggs, she looked at me and said, "Mommy, why are they dipping rocks?" I realized that she didn't even know what an egg was because she'd never seen one!* -- Carianne

Easter egg hunts. What about Easter egg hunts? Sometimes people have their own hunts or go to parks or church events where hunts are sponsored. If they're hunting real eggs, you may not want to partake. If the kids are hunting plastic eggs, let them have the experience. It's fun. If the plastic eggs are filled with non-vegan treats, be sure you have a substitute ready for your kids.

My sister, President of our local Junior Chamber of Commerce, invited me and my two-year-old daughter to an Easter Egg Hunt in the park which was part of an event sponsored by her organization. I wanted to support the event, and I also wanted my daughter to enjoy participating in her first Easter egg hunt. But my sister told me that the plastic eggs were going to contain candies that were non-vegan. I went prepared. I put a large handful of my daughter's favorite animal cookies into a plastic bag, which I kept in my pocket. When it came time for the hunt, my daughter toddled out with all the other kids her age and delighted in picking up the colored eggs and dropping them into her basket. When she wasn't looking, I quickly emptied the eggs of their non-vegan candy, inserted my animal cookies, and put the eggs back together and into her basket. Later, she had the joy of discovering that the eggs could open! Out came her favorite cookies. She was so delighted. While the other kids were snacking on their non-vegan candy, my child was happily munching on her cookies, completely unaware that she was having a different experience than the other kids. We even had other kids complain that their eggs didn't contain cookies! What this taught me as a parent was that I don't have to avoid situations that aren't perfectly vegan; I just have to make sure to have substitutes handy.

Trick-or-treating. I must admit that Halloween was my favorite holiday as a child. At what other time could you spend hours collecting free candy? I figured that when I went vegan and had kids, they would never be able to trick-or-treat. But I was wrong. In 2001, I took my two-year-old daughter out trick-or-treating with a friend who had a five-year-old and a three-year-old, and we all had a blast!

The younger ones can dress up in costumes and go trick-or-treating. When you get home, sort through the bag and pull out all the vegan candies. Then either throw the non-vegan candy away or donate it to a women's shelter so they can give it to their kids.

For older kids who might be off trick-or-treating with their friends, be sure to tell them not to eat anything that you haven't approved first. This should be done regardless of whether a child is vegan! When they get home remove the non-vegan candy, or let them trade it for the vegan candy their friends have, and get rid of the rest. My guess is that non-vegan friends will be glad to have chocolate in exchange for some of their vegan candy.

Also note that while trick-or-treating, sometimes people offer vegan and non-vegan candy in the same bowl. This is great because you can select the vegan candy instead of just taking what you get.

You can also participate in trick-or-treating by giving out vegan candy. Ideas include raisins, peanuts, most hard candies, foil-covered vegan chocolate, coins, and lollipops. For a list of vegan candy, see <u>www.vegfamily.com/lists/</u> <u>vegan-candy.htm</u>.

Halloween parties. Halloween parties can be just as fun for vegan kids as they are for non-vegan kids. Here are some ideas for what to do if your child is invited to a non-vegan Halloween party, and how to throw a great vegan Halloween party yourself.

If your child is going to a non-vegan Halloween party, find out what the hosts will be serving. Send along something similar, and also send a batch of cookies, cupcakes, or other treats that your child can share with the kids at the party. Make sure your child is going to have enough to eat, or send him with a full belly. Most of the fun of going to a Halloween party is dressing up in costume, bobbing for apples, and watching scary movies.

If you decide to throw a Halloween party, you can serve all vegan foods! Make cupcakes and put plastic spiders, ghosts, or pumpkins on top. Carve pumpkins. Serve vegan snack foods like chips, fruit, cut up veggies, and nuts. Serve vegan drinks like fruit punch, apple cider, and natural sodas. Bobbing for apples is vegan already. Create a haunted house for the kids, rent scary movies and serve popcorn. The kids will have a blast!

Chapter 7

TRAVELING

There will come a time when you and your family will do some traveling. Is it hard to be vegan while traveling? Not really. But planning ahead and being prepared will enable you to have some wonderful meals no matter where, or how, you travel. Following are some guidelines for traveling to hotels, taking road trips, going on cruises, getting a vegan meal on an airplane, and finding vegan meals at amusement parks. I'll also explain what to do when traveling to a foreign country.

Hotels

No matter how you travel, when you get to your destination you'll likely be staying at a hotel, inn, or bed & breakfast. It will be helpful to know in advance whether the hotel can accommodate guests with vegan diets. Here are some tips for making your hotel stay a pleasant one.

Look for vegan hotels. Vegan inns and bed & breakfasts are springing up all over the world. If you're flexible on location, start with those. You'll usually get a vegan breakfast and dinner, and some places offer a picnic lunch as well. To find one, do a search online for "vegan bed & breakfasts."

Pick a hotel that offers vegan-friendly fare. If you can't find a vegan hotel, try to find a hotel that at least offers vegan-friendly fare. To do that, check Web sites of hotels in those areas. Some will show the menus for their restaurants. If so, scan the menus for vegetarian and vegan items. Pick the hotel that looks like it offers the widest range of vegan foods.

You can also call ahead and find out if the hotel restaurant staff will be able to accommodate your diet. Don't forget that you can concoct vegan meals using ingredients that you see on the menu. Don't be afraid to ask for something special.

Bring non-perishable snacks. It's a good idea to bring some non-perishable snacks with you to a hotel, especially if it's an extended stay. You can make a decent breakfast out of bagels, dried fruit, dry cereal, and nuts.

Find out if the room will have a coffee maker. Many hotels put coffee makers in their rooms so guests can make coffee or tea. If your hotel does this, you'll be able to make simple foods in your room using hot (bottled) water, such as oatmeal, miso soup, hummus (from a box), and refried beans (also from a box). For a quick, nutritious snack, bring crackers or bread and spread hummus or beans on them.

Book a hotel near vegan restaurants or health food stores. If at all possible, when you're selecting a hotel, pick one that is close to a veg restaurant or health food store. That way, even if the hotel can't accommodate your diet, you'll have somewhere to eat or buy food. Plus, if your stay will be long, you'll want the variety.

Ask for a refrigerator. Some hotels offer their guests an in-room refrigerator, either for free or for a nominal charge. If you can get a refrigerator in your room, then you can stock it with some perishable items like vegan cream cheese for your bagels, soymilk for your cereal, fruit juice, and leftovers from restaurants.

> **Real Stories from Real Parents:**
> *I got the idea to ask for a refrigerator in our hotel when I was pregnant with my second child. I was borderline diabetic and needed to eat at regular intervals. I told the hotel manager my situation and he gave us a refrigerator to use free of charge. Having that refrigerator made all the difference on our trip. We were able to have breakfast in our room every morning and store leftovers in the refrigerator overnight. Now we ask for a refrigerator no matter where we travel. Sometimes we're charged for it and sometimes it's free. It never hurts to ask!* – Yana

Road Trips

Preparation is key when planning a road trip, especially if you're traveling with children. Here are some tips to make your trip fun for everyone.

Plan your route in advance. Before you even get in the car, be sure you know where you're going to stop for the night and where you're going to stop to eat. You don't want to end up eating french fries and dry salad everywhere you go. If possible, go online and find some vegan restaurants along your travel route and plan on stopping there for meals.

Keep non-perishable snacks in the car at all times. You never know when your toddler is going to suddenly become hungry. You could be nowhere near a restaurant or grocery store. Be sure that you've placed some non-perishable foods in the car, such as nuts, dried fruit, non-juicy fruit (like bananas and apples), energy bars, fruit leather, crackers, juice boxes, popcorn, and dry cereal. Beware foods that are choking hazards for your little ones. It's safer to stop the car when snacking because there's less chance of them choking.

Buy what you need in each city. Know in advance where the health food stores along your route are going to be. If your kids are sick of crackers and french fries, a health food store can be a nice change of pace. You may be able to get a grilled vegetable sandwich, garden salad, baked potato, cheeseless pizza, or items from their deli counter such as mock chicken salad, vegan potato salad, or tempeh salad. You could also buy a loaf of bread and sandwich fixings at the store, drive to a nearby park, and have an impromptu picnic!

Cruises

What do you picture when you think of cruises? The food! It's everywhere. Cruises can be a lot of fun, but you don't want to get out to sea and find out that the only thing you'll be eating is fruit, veggies, and rice. What should you do to make sure your cruise experience has the same culinary excitement that other guests enjoy?

Call ahead to arrange special meals. Call the cruise line, tell them you are a vegan, and ask if they can accommodate your diet. Don't just take their word for it, though; make sure they understand what you want. Be prepared to give them some ideas for meals, and don't forget about dessert. Give them the names of a few vegan ice cream products and vegan cookie companies. Some cruise chefs will go the extra mile for you and design a menu that will make other guests swoon with envy. However, some chefs will assume that veggies and rice make a great meal seven nights a week.

Confirm your meal request three days before setting sail. Three days before you're due to set sail, contact the person responsible for your meals and make sure they're going to have everything in time. The last thing you need is to be halfway to your first port only to find that your special food items were never brought on the ship. (If this does happen, ship personnel might be able to buy what they need for you at the next port.)

Book a vegetarian or vegan cruise. If you really want great meals and great service while on a cruise, find a vegetarian cruise – yes, they do exist! Usually the person or travel agent in charge of booking the cruise will be able to pre-approve a menu for the group, ensuring that you'll be getting more than just salad and steamed vegetables. It's also a great way to meet other vegetarians.

If you can't find a vegetarian cruise, get your own vegetarian group together. You'll probably get discount rates. Elect someone from your party to request special meals for the group. The cruise will be more likely to accommodate a large group of people than just one family.

Bring snacks for your family. As with other modes of travel, bring non-perishable vegan snacks for your family – it's good to be prepared for the unexpected. You may especially want to bring vegan desserts since those will be the hardest items to find on a cruise unless arrangements have been made in advance.

Airplanes

You might think it's easy to get a vegan meal on a flight, but the experiences of many vegan travelers would suggest otherwise. Sure, it's easy to *request* a vegan meal; it's just difficult to actually get one. Of the parents I spoke to on this subject, 80% had had at least one experience where they believed they would be getting a vegan meal on their flight but did not. Following are tips and advice to make sure you and your kids don't go hungry on your flight.

Request a vegan meal. This may be a lot harder than it sounds. If you're booking your flight with a travel agent, she will probably make the request for you. But beware – she may select "vegetarian" instead of vegan if she is not clear on the difference. You need to explain your needs very clearly to your agent, and even then there's a chance that you won't get what you require.

If you're not working with a travel agent, call the airline directly to book your flight so that you can discuss options with a real person. Do not use the Internet to book your flight because the meal options may be obscure, you won't be able to ask questions or clarify options, and you won't really know if the person who needs the information has actually received it.

Selecting an option. The variety of meal options on airlines has increased considerably. Here are just some of the choices you have: lacto-ovo-vegetarian, vegan, non-dairy vegetarian, strict vegetarian, Indian vegetarian, raw food, kosher, fruit plate, pure vegetarian, Asian vegetarian, vegetarian, Hindu, Shinto vegetarian, vegetarian without milk, and the list goes on and on. Some people just order a fruit plate, but sometimes that comes with a dollop of cottage cheese on top. Some people order non-dairy, but their meals may contain honey or eggs. You can try asking a customer service representative to explain exactly what is in the meal, but he probably won't know for sure.

Years ago on a flight to Atlanta, my husband and I ordered a vegan meal. We got vegetable lasagna with no cheese, but the margarine for the roll contained whey and the salad dressing contained anchovies. I've heard many stories from travelers who have requested vegan meals and ended up with non-vegan side dishes, no dessert, or their meal was never put on the plane. The bottom line is, don't assume that just because you ordered a vegan meal that you're going to get one.

Confirm your meal ahead of time. Forty-eight hours before your flight, call the airline customer service number and confirm that your meal is scheduled to be on your flight. Then, when you get on the plane, immediately tell the flight attendants that you requested a vegan meal and ask if they can make sure it's on the plane. If not, and you're there early enough, there may still be time to get a vegan meal to the plane before it takes off.

Bring your own food. You never know what's going to happen when you travel by air. Maybe your meal never made it on the plane. Maybe your plane will be delayed.

Recently, my husband had a stopover in Texas while traveling for business. When he boarded the plane for the second leg of his journey, there was a technical problem which resulted in a delay of three hours on the tarmac. The flight attendants passed out all the snacks they had, but everyone was getting hungry – everyone except my husband. He was happily munching on the emergency vegan snacks I packed for him. Be safe, not sorry. Be sure you've got plenty of snacks in your carry-on bag, especially if you have little ones traveling with you.

If your meal is not on the plane. If you requested a vegan meal and didn't get it, or you received a meal that wasn't entirely vegan, write a letter of complaint to the airline. They may send you a voucher or partial refund for your trouble. Also, it tells the airlines that they need to improve their service to vegans. They may think everything is satisfactory if no one complains to them, so make your voice heard.

If you miss your flight. What if your flight is cancelled or you get bumped off the plane? What if you arrive late and miss your flight? When you get on another flight your vegan meal will not be on that plane. Another good reason to have snacks with you! Always plan for the worst and hope for the best.

Amusement Parks

Planning a trip to Disney World or Universal Studios? Just as it's important to plan your route in a road trip or find a hotel that can accommodate your diet, it's a good idea to get advance information about the food offered at amusement parks. Do you really want to leave the park in the middle of the day just to find vegan food? Here are some tips to make sure your day is a culinary delight.

Check the Web site. Popular amusement parks and attractions will have a Web site, so start there. See if you can find menus for their restaurants. Scan the menus for items you can eat, or that can be easily modified. Be aware that food in amusement parks is often pre-assembled and can't be easily altered. For example, if you find a garden salad it may come with chopped hard-boiled eggs and it will be nearly impossible to pick them out.

Call the guest relations department. Large amusement parks will have guest relations staffs. Call them and discuss your dietary needs, and ask if they can accommodate you. Be aware that they may think vegetarian and vegan are the same things, so make your requests clear.

Ask the restaurant managers to accommodate you. Since amusement parks attract people of so many different cultures, you can be reasonably certain that the restaurant managers have at least heard of vegans and know what vegan means. They may be able to create a special meal for you and your family. Don't be afraid to ask.

Bring a picnic lunch or snacks. If you don't want to pay $2.00 for an apple or $5.00 for french fries, bring your own lunch or snacks. You can bring a full cooler and store it in your car (if you're willing to walk all the way back for it), or bring a smaller cooler and store it in one of the lockers that the park offers. You can carry a backpack full of non-perishable snacks, or you can give everyone their own sack lunch to carry. Many people want to maximize their time in an amusement park, so instead of breaking for lunch, they just eat snacks all day while standing in line. What a great use of downtime!

Be prepared for disappointment. One day I called the guest relations department at Disneyland and asked an agent which of their restaurants offered vegan food. She consulted her list and read off at least four restaurants in the park that offered something vegan. Great! There was only one problem. When we got to the park, all of those restaurants were closed! As it turns out, Disneyland closes some of their restaurants on low traffic days, and we had gone on a weekday in the middle of winter – a low traffic day! We spent the day eating french fries and high priced fruit. We still go on weekdays in winter (when the line is sometimes so short that you're the only people on the ride), but we bring our own snacks now. The point is to be prepared for any eventuality. Always have snacks you can eat in an emergency.

Traveling to a Foreign Country
Planning a trip to a foreign country? Traveling outside of your native country can be exciting, but challenging as well, especially if you don't speak the native language. How will you find vegan restaurants? How will you explain to servers that you don't eat animal products? What about hidden ingredients and misunderstandings? Here are some tips to make traveling to a foreign country an easy and pleasant experience.

     Pick a veg-friendly city. It's probably a lot easier to eat vegan in Los Angeles than Moscow. If your travel plans are open, and you're just looking for a place to vacation for a week, select a city that offers a lot of veg-friendly restaurants.

     Pick a veg-friendly hotel. You should select a hotel that offers veg-friendly fare, even if you plan on eating most of your meals outside the hotel. There is always a possibility that bad weather or a strange circumstance will keep you confined to your hotel.

     In 1993 I was at a business convention in Florida. I was just getting ready to leave the hotel to go sightseeing when the hotel manager came over the loud speaker. He said no one was allowed to leave the hotel because deadly mosquitoes, whose bite causes encephalitis, were swarming in the area. All of the guests were stuck inside the hotel for three days while the situation was investigated.

Other people I've spoken with have reported that while vacationing they were confined to their hotels due to hurricane warnings, tornadoes, and blizzards. I've also heard of people confined due to civil unrest in parts of the world where war was imminent. So, pick a hotel that contains food you can eat in case you're unexpectedly there for the long haul.

Pick some restaurants in advance. You've picked your city and your hotel; now it's time to choose some restaurants. There are several guides available that contain lists of vegetarian and vegan restaurants in just about every major city in the world. Buy such a guide and make sure the restaurants you're planning to go to are still in business. You can also find a list of vegan and vegetarian restaurants at www.vegdining.org.

Know where the natural foods stores are. Maybe you're renting a villa or a town home in the country you're visiting. If it has a kitchen, then you're really in luck! Find a health food store nearby and do some grocery shopping. Then you can make your own vegan meals, which will save money as well!

Get recommendations online. If you're not sure where to go or where to eat once you get to your destination, look for recommendations online. The Internet is a wonderful place to plan a veg-friendly vacation. Vegan message boards are great places to find recommendations for places to shop, stay, and eat. If you happen to get responses from people indigenous to the area you plan to visit, you'll end up with the inside scoop on the best veg places in town.

Have a list of key phrases available when eating out. When you sit down in a restaurant you can avoid misunderstandings if you can tell the server – in his own language – exactly what you can and cannot eat. Before you travel, get a list of common phrases in the native language. Learn how to say them, or be prepared to show the server the written phrases. If you can't pronounce the words, just show them to the server. If you visit http://babelfish.altavista.com, you can get phrases translated into many languages.

Beware hidden ingredients. You also need to be careful of hidden ingredients. Rice may be made with chicken stock. Something described as vegetarian on the menu may contain fish sauce. Soups and vegetable stir-fries may contain beef or chicken stock. Just because something looks vegan on the surface, doesn't mean it is. Ask questions.

Beware misunderstandings. Even when it seems like you've been very clear, mistakes can happen. For example, once my husband and I were eating in an Indian restaurant. The server seemed to understand that we didn't eat meat or dairy products and made recommendations which were delicious. We found out later that one of the dishes contained ghee (clarified butter). At a Mexican restaurant in Los Angeles, I ordered a vegetarian tostada and asked them to hold the cheese and sour cream. I found out on my next visit that the beans had pork fat in them. When I asked why they included beans laden with pork fat in their *vegetarian* tostada our server said that pork *was* vegetarian. Sometimes it's better to ask the server what's in a food, let him tell you all the ingredients, and then *you* decide whether you can eat it.

Keep snacks handy. I'm sure this goes without saying, but it's a wise person who keeps a lot of non-perishable snacks handy when traveling to foreign countries. Some countries will not allow you to bring any food across the border, so you may have to find some vegan snacks when you arrive there. Having snacks in a purse or backpack is great when wandering around a city looking for a place to eat. It can take hours to find a vegan restaurant, and you don't want hungry kids nagging at you the whole time.

Know the locations of health food stores. Acquire a guide to natural foods stores in the country you'll be visiting. Or ask your online vegan friends where to shop. When you arrive at your destination, take a quick trip to the store and stock up on non-perishable food items for your trip.

Take a vegan tour. A great way to travel to a new country is to go with a group of vegans, or sign up for a vegan or vegetarian tour. With tours, your guide has already done the legwork for you and will ensure that you receive vegan meals. Plus, your guide will be available to ask detailed questions in the native language *and* is able to understand the responses!

Contact the Vegetarian or Vegan Society. A good idea before traveling to any country is to contact the Vegetarian or Vegan Society and ask them for advice and information about the area in which you'll be traveling. They will be great resources for you, and may be able to point you in the direction of some great restaurants, tours, and hotels.

Real Stories from Real Parents:
My husband and I travel frequently through Europe with our baby, and we've managed to stay very healthy. Even when other people were falling down sick at embassies, we've managed to remain healthy. Soon we'll be traveling through Europe and North to West Africa with a camera crew. We may have to live off of couscous and rice for 3 weeks, but we'll still be vegans. – Shawn

---

Chapter 8

COMPASSION IN ACTION

Raising vegan children is an act of compassion. Guided by you, your children can be tremendous sources of positive change on this planet. They can be an example to other children of how to live peacefully with animals and how to live in harmony with nature. There is no greater gift you can give your children than the gift of a compassionate soul. Following are ways you and your children can help the animals and protect the environment. You'll learn how to protest positively; meaning safely, without violence, and without causing harm to other people or their property.

Helping the Animals
Animals cannot speak for themselves. They cannot complain about their living conditions or the poor treatment they receive from humans. As vegans, it is our responsibility to speak for animals, to work actively to end their suffering, and to help educate others about what is tolerable and what is simply unacceptable. Following are just a few of the ways in which you and your children can help the animals.

     Avoid cruel amusements. Rodeos, circuses, marine parks, bullfighting, horse racing, and zoos are some of the places where animals are held in captivity and forced to provide entertainment for people. Consider that Orcas, or killer whales, could live to be 100 years old in the wild, but when pressed to perform in a marine park may live only 18 months to 20 years. Zoos often sell off their old animals to game parks where people can pay to shoot them. If enough people would stop patronizing these businesses, they would have no choice but to shut down. If you want your children to see real, live animals, either visit an animal rescue or view animals in their natural habitats without disturbing them and without forcing them to perform.

Rescue, don't buy. If your family decides to bring a companion animal into the home, adopt one from an animal shelter instead of buying one at a pet store. Pet stores are in business to make money, and often the animals in those stores are treated poorly and not cared for with love and attention. Pet stores also sell animals that should not be domesticated, such as ferrets, fishes, and turtles. Pet stores often get their animals through forced breeding programs. Why force animals to breed when there are so many already who need homes?

If you notice animals in your mall's pet store who are sick, mistreated, or living in dirty cages with dirty food and water, tell someone. Write a letter documenting the abuse to the owner of the mall. Ask that they not renew the pet store owner's lease. Write to your local Better Business Bureau, humane society, and especially the A.S.P.C.A (which has a "report animal cruelty section" on their Web site). Also write a letter to the owner of the pet store asking him to find another business. Do not physically disrupt the pet store's operations, or you may face arrest or a fine. People don't respect terrorists; they respect diplomats.

Spay and neuter. If you do rescue an animal from a shelter, make sure it is spayed or neutered before you take him or her home. If you rescue a stray animal, get him or her to the veterinarian and spayed or neutered as soon as possible. Every year millions of animals are put to death because they do not have homes.

Should you let your companion animals have babies? Is it OK to let your cat have kittens if you know you can find good homes for every one of them? Well consider this: for every new kitten who enters our world and finds a home, another homeless cat is condemned to death. If you think you can find good homes for your cat's kittens, consider using those homes for stray kittens or cats, which you can find at a shelter. If you want more animals in your life, rescue more of them from shelters; don't breed them.

Keep your companion animals safe. Be certain to put identifying tags on your companion animals so that they can be returned to you easily if they are lost. If your cats or dogs end up in a shelter because they didn't have a tag, they could tragically be destroyed before you have a chance to find them.

Take several pictures of your animal friend when you first get him, in case he gets lost and you need to put his picture on a flyer.

If your companion animal does get lost, move quickly to find him. Post flyers on telephone poles and at the library, contact local veterinarians in case he was brought there after an accident, and give a picture of him to all the shelters in your area so they can be on the lookout for your animal. In addition, ask neighbors to keep an eye out for him.

Treat your companion animals well. If you decide to give your child a companion animal as a gift, be certain that the child is ready and willing to take of her properly, always remembering that *you* are also responsible for the well-being of that animal. Buy books about how to take care of that kind of animal, and make sure you are providing her a good home, with lots of room to move around, and plenty of fresh, clean water and food. That animal is your family's responsibility for life. Be sure you want the responsibility *before* you take it. Remember, your children will eventually move out, and you may be caring for this animal for the rest of its life. Be sure that everyone in the family is willing and able to adopt this animal.

Get your companion animal a companion. Animals enjoy the company of other animals. Are you going to be at work all day while the kids are at school? If you can support two animals, do it, but make sure they are compatible.

Support animal rescues. If you're looking for a place to donate money or time, consider animal rescues. These places need money and support to provide food, shelter, and medical care to the animals in their charge.

Buy cruelty-free products. One of the best ways to help the animals is to avoid buying products that contain animal ingredients or that were tested on animals. You can find cruelty-free versions of just about every product you will need, including household cleaners, detergents, shampoos, soaps, and lotions. Avoid buying clothing made from animals, such as leather, silk, fur, feathers, wool, and snakeskin. Confirm that your jewelry is not made of ivory or bone. Make sure your perfume or cologne was not tested on animals and that it is not made of musk. If you can't find cruelty-free products in your health food store, shop online at one of the many vegan businesses that offer alternatives to common items.

Protecting the Environment

One reason people go vegan is to help protect the environment. When you stop eating animal products, you are making a direct impact on preserving the natural resources of our planet. There are some actions you can take every day to save the planet.

Recycle. I'm sure you're already aware of how important it is to recycle. We have two trash cans in our kitchen: one for garbage and one for recyclables. In our neighborhood, three trucks come by once a week; one picks up garbage, one picks up all our recyclables (we don't have to sort them by type), and one picks up lawn trimmings. At least 40% of our trash each week is recyclable. If everyone recycled 40% of their garbage, imagine how much room that would save in the landfills! Here is a partial list of things you can recycle:

- Toner cartridges (sent to companies who specialize in recycling these products)
- Aluminum cans
- Newspapers
- Plastic bottles
- Soymilk cartons
- Glass
- Telephone books
- Paper

Stop junk mail. Did you know that up to half of junk mail is never opened! Even if you recycle it, there are other costs to the environment, such as ink, the energy to produce and deliver the paper, and the loss of virgin forest used to create the junk mail in the first place. But there's a solution. Did you know you can prevent junk mail from coming to your home? Here are some tips:

Call 1-888-OPT-OUT to prevent credit card companies from selling your information to other companies. Your credit card company is responsible for most of the junk mail you are receiving.

Be wary of entering mail in contests. It's likely that the company sponsoring the contest will use your name, address, and phone number to send you junk mail, or sell your info to other companies.

Send a letter to *DMA Mail Preference Service, P.O. Box 9008, Farmingdale, NY 11735-9008*. Include your complete name, address, zip code and a request to "activate the preference service." You will need to do this for all the spellings of your name (i.e., J. Doe, Jane Doe, J.A. Doe, etc.) For up to five years, this will stop mail from all member organizations that you have not specifically ordered products from. Note that this option may stop catalogs and promotions you would have liked to receive.

When you donate money, order a product or service, or fill out a warranty card, write the following on it in bold letters: "Please do not sell my name or address." Most companies will honor your request.

If you're giving someone information over the telephone, be sure to ask that they not sell or trade your personal information. Ask them to mark your account accordingly.

To stop supermarkets from mailing you their weekly specials, contact the store's customer service department and ask to be taken off their list.

Store leftovers in plastic containers. Instead of using plastic wrap or aluminum foil to store your food leftovers, use plastic containers, which you can wash and reuse many times.

Use rechargeable batteries. Batteries contain cadmium and mercury. We don't want those getting dumped into landfills! Switch to rechargeable batteries, and recycle alkaline batteries if you can.

Use canvas shopping bags. When you go grocery shopping, bring a few canvas bags and use them to bag your groceries. Some stores will even give you a nickel for every bag that you supply.

Keep major appliances clean and in good working order. Your water heater, refrigerator, and air conditioner use a lot of energy. Keep them in good working order by following manufacturer recommendations on cleaning filters and clearing out accumulated sediment.

Keep your tires properly inflated. This will save gas and also prevent having to replace your tires so often.

Use low flush toilets. A lot of the water that goes down with a flush isn't necessary. You can put a bottle filled with water or stones in your toilet tank to displace some of the water used to flush. Or you can buy a dam at your local hardware store, which will block off part of the tank.

Recycle your motor oil. If you get your oil changed at a gas station, make sure they recycle the used oil. If you do it yourself, take the oil to a gas station or oil-changing service outlet that will recycle it for you. Dumping oil into the sewer system pollutes our waters and injures marine life.

Use fluorescent lighting. Instead of incandescent bulbs, switch to fluorescent lighting. The initial cost is higher, but the bulbs last many times longer than incandescent bulbs.

Use cloth diapers. Over 18 billion disposable diapers end up in landfills each year. Although people are supposed to rinse them out, only 5% actually do. There is also a potential for adding more disease to our groundwater. A disposable diaper takes 500 years to decompose and you can only use it once. A cloth diaper takes one to six months to decompose and can be used 100 times.

If you prefer disposable diapers, there are environmentally friendly versions that may be just the compromise you're seeking. Search the Internet for environmentally friendly disposable diapers and you'll find several companies that offer excellent options.

Buy products that are recycled. Look for books, magazines, and newspapers printed with recycled paper. Also choose products that are sold in containers that are recycled and recyclable.

Save gas. Give the car a break, and carpool, walk, or ride a bike whenever you can.

Buy in bulk. When possible, buy products in bulk, which saves packaging materials and energy.

Reuse whatever you can. Items that can be used again include plastic cutlery, aluminum pie tins, and glass jars.

Reuse scratch paper. If you print something from your computer and don't need it, keep it in a stack and use the back as scratch paper or reuse in your printer.

These are just some of the ways you can help the environment. See how many other ideas you and your family can come up with.

Positive Protesting

I believe in positive protesting, which to me means using education, example, and non-violent means to make people aware that they are harming their health, the environment, and the rights of animals by their behavior. I don't understand groups that physically attack people in the name of peace.

I believe that if you really want to make a difference in the world, you must begin with yourself. I saw a great bumper sticker that read: "Be in the world what you want to see in the world." Let's teach our children how to make lasting, welcome changes on our planet. Following are some ways you and your children can have a positive impact on your community and your planet.

Write letters. "The pen is mightier than the sword." How often have we heard that? Well, it's true. Teach your children that when they experience an injustice, or when they see cruelty, they can do something about it. They can write to a congressperson or politician and ask them to vote vegan. They can write to presidents of companies and ask them to stop testing their products on animals. They can ask fast food companies to carry vegan options. They can ask school officials to do away with mandatory dissection in the classroom, or ask the cafeteria to serve vegan options. They can write to their local paper and express their opinions (who knows, it might get published). If your child is feeling frustrated by an injustice, suggest writing a letter. As Margaret Mead put it, "Never doubt that a small group of thoughtful, committed citizens can change the world; indeed, it's the only thing that ever has."

Make phone calls. Similar to writing letters, your kids can make a difference by using the phone. Urge them to call the toll free numbers of companies that produce products that were tested on animals or that contain animal ingredients. They can also call companies that make vegetarian foods and ask whether they can make vegan versions. Without demand, there will be no supply. Teach your children the importance of speaking up and asking for what they want.

Partake in surveys or public opinion polls. Recently my husband and I were leaving Universal Studios in Los Angeles and one of the employees asked if he could give us a quick, five-minute survey to find out how we enjoyed our day. Although we were tired and wanted to get home, I recognized this as an opportunity to share our experience. We went into a nice office and spent ten minutes (not five!) telling the surveyor that there weren't enough vegan options in the restaurants, and that several restaurant managers weren't even sure what the word vegan meant! We made some suggestions about what they could serve and how it would benefit the many diverse cultures that visit their park. Will anything change? Maybe, maybe not. But if we didn't tell them what we wanted, how would decision-makers ever know, and how would things ever change?

Table events. You don't have to be a member of a large organization to pass out information to people passing by. You can set up a table with literature, brochures, and information in front of a grocery store, at a concert, in front of a circus, at a zoo, at an environmental festival, or wherever people gather. Before you set up a table, be sure you've received permission from the proper authority: the city if you're on public property, the owner if you're on private property.

When you table, be sure not to harass people who aren't interested in your information. Don't waste your breath on those who are looking for a fight; save it for people who are open to what you're saying. When you table with children, be sure you are in a safe place.

Picketing. Picketing a business can be an intense experience. Be sure that if you bring your children with you that you are in a safe place, during the day, with lots of people around. Also make sure that things are not likely to get ugly and turn violent. Even the most well-intentioned groups can end up in physical conflict. Never damage or deface someone's property, since that's against the law. Getting arrested might get you noticed, but it's not the way to make change.

Hold fundraisers. Fundraising is fun. It can be as simple as having a lemonade stand, or as elaborate as organizing a charity ball for people in your community. Let your kids come up with ideas for fundraisers and let them decide where to donate the money they make.

Here are some ideas to get you started: have a bake sale, organize a garage sale, go door-to-door asking for donations, mow people's lawns, sell crafts, or create and sell gift baskets during the holidays. They'll have some fun and help a good cause too!

Organize cleanup days. Cleanup days are great fun for kids and great for the environment too. All you need are a bunch of kids (and adults) and a place to clean. You can tidy up the neighborhood, the beach, a park, or a school. Spend some time cleaning, picking up trash, and beautifying the place. Then celebrate over vegan pizza. Wear special t-shirts that signify your group or organization. Other people in the area may join in, or you may get some press from the local newspaper. Contact newspapers a few weeks before the event to see if they will announce it in their community sections. That way others can participate.

Support vegan businesses. One of the best ways to make a difference is to buy from businesses selling vegan products. First and foremost, look for companies whose product line is totally vegan. Companies that produce entirely vegan product lines are at a disadvantage when their competition is selling to vegetarians and omnivores. It's difficult for all-vegan companies to succeed because vegans are such a small percentage of the population. I've seen too many great vegan products disappear from the market due to lack of sales. Therefore, it's vital to support them as often as you can.

There are some companies that sell vegan *and* non-vegan products. People often ask me if they should support those companies since they don't want their money going to companies that sell meat or dairy products. My view is that the more vegan products these companies sell, the more likely they are to continue making these and new vegan products. Take Gardenburger for example. When they started they were selling vegetarian patties. Today they sell several vegan products that are delicious! Companies respond to consumer demand. Let them know what you want by buying their vegan products often.

Boycott cruel companies. There are some companies whose practices simply cannot be sanctioned by vegans. Don't buy their products. Write letters to newspapers and send messages to Web discussion groups asking other people to boycott them, and tell your friends and family as well. If enough people boycott a company or product, they will make changes. Businesses need customers or they will be out of business. Take away their customers by using the truth to expose them.

Ninety-nine percent dairy free. I am frequently asked if we should consume products that are 99% dairy-free, or that contain trace amounts of dairy. You may wonder why a company would make a product that's so close to being vegan but not go all the way. One reason is that using dedicated machinery is extremely expensive. Most companies manufacture their products on machines that are also manufacturing products for other companies. Although the machines are thoroughly cleaned between batches, they cannot say that their products are 100% dairy free because the possibility exists that someone with a severe milk allergy could become sick. That's why you'll also notice warnings on packages that say, "May contain trace amounts of nuts," since some people who are allergic to nuts can have a severe reaction even with only trace amounts. If you have a severe milk allergy, you should avoid eating items that say 99% dairy-free.

Many start-up vegan companies simply can't afford to manufacture their products on dedicated machinery. It's up to you whether you want to eat the item or not, but for all intents and purposes, the product is vegan. Since going vegan, I've seen several companies who previously made their products on shared machines now make products on dedicated machinery. If consumers hadn't bought enough of these products when they were 99% dairy-free, we wouldn't have them 100% dairy-free today. Something to think about.

Sharing in school. A great way for your kids to help spread the vegan message is for them to incorporate it into their schoolwork whenever possible. For example, if they are required to give a speech, they can talk about being vegan or helping the environment. They can write plays about rescuing animals or being vegan, and then ask the teacher if they can put the play on for the school or classroom. In addition, they can write about being vegan in essays.

For "show and tell," your child can bring in the empty boxes from foods he likes and show the other kids the great variety of vegan products available. If it's feasible, he can also bring in samples of foods for the other children to try. Another idea is to arrange for animal rescue workers to bring in some of their animals and show the children how to properly treat them.

Share your culture. Be an example to your child's friends. When they come over, offer healthy and delicious vegan snacks. Let them ask you questions about being vegan. If you're up to it, give a talk in your child's classroom about what it means to be a vegan. Explain how you are teaching your child to be compassionate and kind to animals. Let them know how they too can make a difference.

Chapter 9

KID-FRIENDLY RECIPES

On the following pages you will find a collection of 32 recipes that are easy to make, delicious, and full of vitamins. They've also passed the toddler test; my daughter loves them all! Most of them come from my favorite cookbooks, and the authors have graciously given their permission to allow me to share them with you. I have contributed some of my best homemade recipes as well.

These recipes are the ones we make frequently in our home. I think that once you try them you'll see why we make them so often!

For more vegan recipes and a list of vegan cookbooks, see www.vegfamily.com/vegan-recipes/index.htm and www.vegfamily.com/book-reviews/index.htm

BREAKFASTS

Pancakes
Reprinted with permission from The Compassionate Cook by PETA and Ingrid Newkirk. www.peta.org

Ingredients:
- 1 cup unbleached all-purpose flour
- 1 tablespoon sugar
- 2 tablespoons baking powder
- 1/8 teaspoon salt
- 1 cup soymilk
- 2 tablespoons vegetable oil

Directions:
Combine the flour, sugar, baking powder, and salt in a bowl and mix thoroughly. Mix in the soymilk and oil, and with an electric mixer or wire whisk, beat just until the batter is smooth.

Measure 1/3 cup batter onto a hot, oiled griddle. When bubbles appear on the upper surface, lift with a spatula and flip the pancake. Cook the pancake for another 2 minutes or until done. Remove from pan and keep warm while you cook remaining pancakes. Serve warm with maple syrup or fruit syrup.

Erin's Comments: You can add blueberries, bananas, or chocolate chips to the pancakes for an added treat!

French Toast

Reprinted with permission from The Compassionate Cook by PETA and
Ingrid Newkirk. www.peta.org

Ingredients:

- 1 1/2 cups soymilk
- 2 tablespoons unbleached all-purpose flour
- 1 tablespoon nutritional yeast
- 1 teaspoon sugar
- 1 teaspoon ground cinnamon
- 1 tablespoon vegetable oil
- 4-6 slices bread (thick-sliced crusty white or wheat bread)

Directions:

Mix the soymilk, flour, yeast, sugar, and cinnamon
vigorously with a wire whisk or beater. Pour the mixture into
a wide, shallow bowl or pie pan.

Heat the oil in a frying pan or skillet. Dip a bread slice into
the milk mixture and then place in skillet. Fry each side until
golden brown and crispy, about 5 to 7 minutes total.

Remove from pan and keep warm while cooking remaining
slices.

Serve hot with maple syrup.

Tip: If you like powdered sugar on your french toast, you
can make some by blending 2 cups of fructose with ½ cup
cornstarch in a high-powered blender.

Tofu Scramble

Reprinted with permission from The Compassionate Cook by PETA and Ingrid Newkirk. www.peta.org

Ingredients:

- 1 pound firm tofu, patted dry and mashed
- 1/8 teaspoon turmeric
- 1 teaspoon onion powder
- 1/2 teaspoon salt
- 1 cup finely chopped vegetables (green bell pepper, fresh mushrooms, onions, tomatoes – whatever you like)

Directions:

Place the tofu in a lightly oiled sauté pan and cook over medium heat for 3 minutes. Add the remaining ingredients, stir well, and cook for 5 to 8 minutes, until the vegetables are cooked and the tofu is heated through.

Erin's Notes: A great, nutritious, fast breakfast that your kids will love.

Did you know? To make tofu scramble even easier, just pick up a box of Tofu Scrambler mix from the health food store. All you have to do is mash firm tofu, mix in the powder, and cook in a skillet for a few minutes. Easy!

Fruit Smoothie
Recipe by Erin Pavlina

Ingredients:
- 2 bananas
- 1 apple
- 1 orange, peeled
- 1 cup of fresh pineapple chunks
- 1-2 cups of frozen strawberries
- 2 cups of apple juice

Directions:
In the order listed, put the ingredients into a high-powered blender, and blend on high until smooth and creamy. Pour into a tall glass and serve with a straw!

Variations:
You can add any fruits to this. The key to making a great smoothie is to use bananas for creaminess, frozen fruit to make it cold and thick like a shake, and fruit juice so it doesn't come out all pulpy.

Drink your vitamins: One glass of fruit smoothie can provide your child with 3 to 4 servings of fruit, plus give her lots of vitamins! I haven't met a child yet who could resist a fruit smoothie. Picky toddlers beware...

BREADS

Lemon Blueberry Muffins
Compliments of Allison Rivers, President of Allison's Gourmet. www.allisonsgourmet.com

Ingredients:
- 3 1/2 cups whole-wheat pastry flour
- 1 tablespoon baking powder
- 1/2 teaspoon baking soda
- 1 teaspoon sea salt
- 1/2 cup sunflower oil
- 2/3 cup maple syrup
- 1/4 cup water
- Juice and zest of one lemon
- 3/4 cup blueberries

Directions:
Heat oven to 400 degrees. Place paper baking cups into muffin tin.

Combine flour, baking powder, baking soda, and sea salt in a large bowl. In a separate bowl, whisk oil, syrup, water, juice, and zest of lemon. Add the wet ingredients to the dry ingredients and blend with a light touch. Mixing too vigorously will result in tough muffins.

Gently fold in blueberries. Quickly pour batter into muffin cups and place in oven. Bake for 20 minutes. Make one dozen muffins.

Erin's Comments: Great with tea or for breakfast. You can substitute other fruits in place of the blueberries or use orange in place of lemon.

Holiday Pumpkin Bread

Reprinted with permission from Incredibly Delicious: The Vegan
Paradigm Cookbook by Gentle World Publishing. www.gentleworld.org

Ingredients:
- 2 1/4 cup whole-wheat pastry flour, sifted
- 1 teaspoon baking soda, sifted
- 1/4 teaspoon sea salt
- 2 1/2 teaspoons Ener-G Egg Replacer
- 2-3 teaspoons cinnamon
- 1 1/2 cups Sucanat (or dry sweetener)
- 1/3 cup oil
- 1 cup pumpkin (canned or fresh, cooked)
- 1/4 cup orange juice
- 1 teaspoon vanilla
- 1/2 cup raisins
- 1/2 cup pecans/walnuts, chopped

Directions:
Sift all the dry ingredients into a bowl and mix. Add oil,
pumpkin, orange juice and vanilla. Mix with a fork. Fold in
raisins and nuts. Mix. Pour into an oiled cake or bread pan.

Bake in a pre-heated oven at 350 degrees for 45-50 minutes
for a cake, 60 minutes for a bread loaf. The bread is done
when a toothpick comes out dry.

Corn Muffins

Reprinted with permission from Eat Your Veggies by Beverly Lynn Bennett. www.veganchef.com

Ingredients:

- 2 tablespoons water
- 1 1/2 teaspoons Ener-G Egg Replacer
- 1 cup soymilk
- 1/4 cup canola oil
- 1 cup cornmeal
- 1 cup unbleached flour
- 4 tablespoons unbleached cane sugar
- 1 tablespoon baking powder
- 1/2 teaspoon salt

Directions:

In a small bowl, whisk egg replacer and water until frothy. Add soymilk and canola oil and whisk well to combine. In a large bowl, combine cornmeal, flour, sugar, baking powder, and salt. Add wet ingredients to the dry ingredients, stirring just enough to mix. Fill greased muffin pans 1/2 to 2/3 full. Bake at 425 degrees for 15 to 20 minutes or until lightly browned. Yields 12 muffins.

Erin's Notes: You can also pour the mixture into a square baking dish and make corn bread. This is fast, it tastes great, and my toddler loves it. Serve hot with some soy margarine for a real treat!

SANDWICHES

Quickie Faux Egg Salad Sandwich
Reprinted with permission from How It All Vegan!: Irresistible Recipes for an Animal-Free Diet by Tanya Barnard and Sarah Kramer
www.GoVegan.net

Ingredients:
- 1/2 cup medium or firm tofu
- 2 – 3 tablespoons vegan mayonnaise
- 1/4 teaspoon turmeric
- 1 tablespoon celery, finely diced
- 1 teaspoon red or green onion, finely diced
- Dash of pepper
- 4 slices of bread
- 1/4 teaspoon Dijon mustard (optional)

Directions:
In a small bowl, mash together the tofu, mayonnaise, and turmeric. Stir in the celery, onions, pepper, and optional mustard. Spread between slices of bread. You can add sprouts, lettuce, grated carrots, or anything else that tickles your fancy.

Garden Hummus Sandwich
Recipe by Erin Pavlina

Ingredients:
- Whole wheat pita bread
- Romaine lettuce
- Tomatoes
- Cucumber slices
- Roasted red pepper hummus (store bought)

Directions:
Slice the top off the pita bread and open it up. Spread 2 tablespoons of hummus on the insides of the bread. Stuff the pocket with lettuce, tomato, and cucumber slices. Serve.

Variations: You can also add falafel, avocado, grated carrots, or onions to this sandwich, depending on your child's tastes.

Erin's Comments: I like to call this our "Vitamin C, protein, calcium, iron sandwich," but don't tell my toddler how good it is for her! She loves the taste of the hummus, the crunch of the veggies, and the softness of the pita.

Grilled Cheese Sandwich
Recipe by Erin Pavlina

Ingredients:
- 2 slices whole wheat bread
- Soy margarine
- 2 slices vegan American cheese

Directions:
Spread a thin layer of margarine on both slices of bread. Put the two slices of cheese between them, with the margarine side out.

Heat sandwich on a pan over medium heat. Keep your spatula pressing down on top so the cheese melts. When the bottom slice of bread is lightly browned, flip the sandwich over and grill the other side. Keep your spatula pressed down the entire time.

Tip: The secret to making good vegan grilled cheese sandwiches is to keep the heat low enough to give the cheese time to melt. If the heat is too high, the bread will burn before the cheese melts.

Chickpea Pita Pockets
Reprinted with permission from Cooking with PETA by PETA. www.peta.org

Ingredients:
- 1 (16 oz.) can chickpeas, rinsed, drained, and mashed
- 1/3 cup chopped celery
- 1 tablespoon minced onion
- 2 tablespoons pickle relish
- 2 tablespoons egg-free mayonnaise
- 1 teaspoon mustard
- Dash of garlic powder (optional)
- 4 whole wheat pitas
- Lettuce, tomato slices, grated carrot, etc., for toppings

Directions:
Place the chickpeas, celery, onion, pickle relish, mayonnaise, mustard, and garlic powder in a bowl, and stir well.

Cut the pitas in half, and open up into pockets. Fill each pita pocket with 1/8 of the chick-pea spread, top with lettuce, tomato slices or other veggies, and serve immediately. For bag lunches, pack the spread, veggies, and pita bread in separate containers. Assemble just before eating.

Erin's Comments: Great flavor, and a little something different than peanut butter and jelly sandwiches!

SIDE DISHES

Steamed Broccoli and Squash
Recipe by Erin Pavlina

Ingredients:
- 2 cups of broccoli, chopped
- 2 cups of butternut squash, cut into 1 inch cubes
- Tamari or soy sauce
- Ginger powder (optional)

Directions:
Steam broccoli and squash until tender. Sprinkle with some tamari and ginger powder. Serve.

Erin's Comments: My daughter loves these two vegetables together because the squash adds a little sweetness to the broccoli. Plus it's fast and easy to make!

Helpful Hint: If you don't have time to peel and cut a butternut squash, buy it pre-cut and pre-cubed at the store. I've often asked someone in the produce section to do this for me and they always have. Saves a ton of time! You can also find broccoli and other veggies pre-cut and ready to be thrown into soups or stews.

Tofu Cottage Cheese
Reprinted with permission from Incredibly Delicious: The Vegan Paradigm Cookbook by Gentle World Publishing. www.gentleworld.org

Ingredients:
- 1 pound firm tofu, drained and mashed
- 2/3 cup vegan mayonnaise
- 1 teaspoon sea salt (optional)
- 2 teaspoons onion powder
- 1 teaspoon garlic powder
- 1 teaspoon caraway seeds

Directions:
Mix all ingredients together in a bowl. Store in refrigerator.

Tip: Use tofu cottage cheese in place of ricotta cheese in your lasagna recipes. You can also use this to make a great vegan Reuben sandwich!

Candied Sweet Potatoes

Reprinted with permission from Eat Your Veggies by Beverly Lynn Bennett. www.veganchef.com

Ingredients:

- 4 lbs. sweet potatoes, washed well
- 1/3 cup maple syrup
- 1/4 cup Sucanat
- 3 tablespoons Spectrum Naturals' Spectrum Spread or non-hydrogenated spreadable margarine.

Directions:

Peel and cut the sweet potatoes into large cubes. Cook sweet potato cubes in a pot of salted boiling water until tender, about 15 minutes. Drain and set aside. In the same pot, combine remaining ingredients and cook over medium heat until the Sucanat is thoroughly dissolved and the mixture starts to bubble. Return the sweet potatoes to the pot and toss with the bubbling syrup to thoroughly coat each cube.

Erin's Comments: Great for holidays or special dinners.

Pasta Salad
Recipe by Erin Pavlina

Ingredients:
- 1 bag of corkscrew pasta
- 1 red bell pepper
- 1 cup of broccoli florets
- 1 cup carrots, chopped
- 2 zucchini, grated
- black olives, chopped (optional)
- Italian dressing

Directions:
Prepare pasta according to package instructions. Drain and set aside until cool.

Add vegetables and toss with Italian dressing to taste. Chill and serve.

Tip: Great salad for potlucks, parties, celebrations, baby showers, etc.

Mashed Potatoes
Recipe by Jane Pavlina

Ingredients:
- 6 red (new) potatoes, medium size (can use russet potatoes)
- 1 stick margarine, cut into pieces
- 1 teaspoon salt
- 1/4 cup soymilk

Directions:
Peel potatoes and cut into 1" cubes. Place in deep pot and cover with water. Bring to a boil and cook until potatoes are soft (poke with fork). Drain.

Place softened potatoes in an electric mixer bowl and add margarine. Beat slowly until there are no lumps, then increase speed to smooth out. Add soymilk and salt. Adjust to desired consistency and taste.

Variations:
- Use onion or garlic salt
- Add vegan bacon bits
- Sprinkle finely chopped parsley on top
- Sprinkle finely chopped green onions on top
- Add minced garlic

Erin's Comments: Pour your favorite vegan gravy on top.

MAIN DISHES

Neat Loaf
Reprinted with permission from Cooking with PETA by PETA.
www.peta.org

Ingredients:
- 1 lb. firm tofu, mashed
- 1/2 cup wheat germ
- 1/3 cup chopped fresh parsley, or 1 ½ tablespoons dried parsley
- 1/4 cup chopped onion, or 1 tablespoon onion powder
- 2 tablespoons soy sauce
- 2 tablespoons nutritional yeast (optional)
- 1/2 tablespoon Dijon mustard
- 1/4 teaspoon garlic powder
- 1/4 teaspoon black pepper
- 2 tablespoons oil

Directions:
Preheat the oven to 350 degrees.

Mix together the ingredients except the oil. Use the oil to coat a loaf pan. Press the tofu mixture into oiled loaf pan, and bake for about 1 hour. Let cool about 10 minutes before removing from the pan. Garnish with ketchup and parsley. This is also good sliced and fried for sandwiches the next day.

Erin's Comments: I can throw this together so fast; in less than five minutes it's in the oven. This recipe rescues me when I need to make something nutritious but don't have time to chop, sauté and stir-fry, etc. And my toddler loves it with ketchup.

Funny-Face Burritos
Reprinted with permission from Cooking with PETA by PETA.
www.peta.org

Ingredients:
- 4 large whole-wheat tortillas
- 1 teaspoon canola oil
- 1/4 yellow onion, diced
- Chili powder to taste (optional)
- 1 (16 oz.) can kidney or pinto beans, rinsed and drained
- 1/4 cup mild salsa

Toppings:
Sliced black olives, cherry tomatoes, red bell pepper strips, cooked corn kernels, shredded lettuce leaves, grated carrots.

Directions:
Wrap the tortillas in foil and warm them in the oven for about 10 minutes.

Meanwhile, heat the oil in a skillet over medium heat. Sauté the onion until softened, about 5 minutes. Add the chili powder and cook for 1 minute. Add the beans and salsa, and cook until the beans are heated through.

Place the bean mixture in a food processor, and puree until smooth.

Spread 1/4 of the bean mixture on each tortilla. Let your kids make faces on the tortillas using the vegetables: for instance, sliced black olives for eyes, a cherry tomato for the nose, red pepper slices for lips, corn kernels for teeth, and shredded lettuce or grated carrots for hair.

Teriyaki Tempeh
Compliments of Allison Rivers, President and Founder of Allison's Gourmet. www.allisonsgourmet.com

Ingredients:
- 1 - 8 ounce package tempeh
- 2 tablespoons sesame oil
- 1/4 cup tamari
- 1/4 cup maple syrup

Directions:
Heat a large skillet. Add the sesame oil, then the tempeh. Sauté until golden brown on both sides. Remove from heat and immediately pour in the tamari and maple syrup completely coating the tempeh as the teriyaki glaze is formed. Extra teriyaki sauce can be made by heating equal amounts of tamari and maple syrup in a small saucepan until medium-thick consistency. Great served with rice and stir-fried vegetables.

Erin's Comments: Delicious and easy! Tempeh has a great texture, and is a great source of vitamins.

Curried Chickpeas

Reprinted with permission from Simply Vegan by Debra Wasserman. www.vrg.org

Ingredients:

- Small onion, chopped
- 1 tablespoon oil
- 19 ounce can chickpeas or garbanzo beans, drained (or 2 cups cooked chickpeas)
- 1 tablespoon curry powder
- 1/4 teaspoon black pepper

Directions:

Sauté onion in oil over medium-high heat for 3 minutes. Add chickpeas and spices and continue heating for 3 more minutes, stirring occasionally. Serve hot with rice and/or steamed kale.

Erin's Comments: If you're worried about it being too spicy for your kids, use a mild curry or cut back on the amount you use. You can also mash the beans and give them to your one-year-old.

> **Did you know?** Chickpeas and garbanzo beans are the same thing.

Eggplant Tomato – Tahini Bake

Reprinted with permission from Incredibly Delicious: The Vegan Paradigm Cookbook by Gentle World Publishing. www.gentleworld.org

Ingredients:

- 2 – 3 eggplants (medium sized)
- 3 ripe red tomatoes (large)
- 1 onion, sliced
- 1 1/4 cup water
- 3/4 cup tahini
- 2 garlic cloves (fresh)
- 1/4 cup nutritional yeast
- 2 tablespoons tamari
- 2 teaspoons salt-free Spike
- Garlic oil for sauté
- 3 cups mushrooms, halved
- 1 tablespoon tamari
- 1/4 cup scallion, diced
- Paprika

Directions:
1. Slice eggplant in thin slices. Slice the tomato and onion.
2. In an oiled casserole dish, place a layer of eggplant covered with a layer of sliced tomato and onion.
3. In a blender, blend water, tahini, garlic, yeast, tamari and Spike.
4. Pour a thin layer of the blended mixture over the layered vegetables. Then add another layer of vegetables along with some more dressing.
5. Fill almost to the top with layers of tomato, onion, eggplant, and sauce, leaving some sauce out for later. Begin baking at 375 degrees in a pre-heated oven.

6. Make some garlic oil in a blender by blending garlic with oil. In a small fry pan, sauté the mushrooms that are cut in half, in the garlic oil. Season with tamari.

7. When eggplant is partially cooked, remove from oven. Mix the mushroom sauté with the sauce saved from step 5. Pour this mixture over the top of the casserole, and spread out evenly. Sprinkle with diced scallions and paprika. Bake until eggplant is melt-in-your-mouth soft, approximately 1 hour.

Variation: Try a zucchini tahini bake. Replace eggplant and tomatoes (if desired) with zucchini and extra onions. This bake will take a little less cooking time and is also rich and delicious.

Erin's Comments: Tahini is high in calcium and gives this dish a nice, creamy consistency. This casserole goes so fast in our house that we often make a double recipe so we can have leftovers.

SNACKS

Maple Apple Dip
Reprinted with permission from How It All Vegan!: Irresistible Recipes
for an Animal-Free Diet by Tanya Barnard and Sarah Kramer
Arsenal Pulp Press
www.GoVegan.net

Ingredients:
- 1 cup silken tofu
- 1/2 teaspoon cinnamon
- 1/2 teaspoon vanilla extract
- 1/4 cup maple syrup
- 1-2 medium apples, sliced

Directions:
In a blender or food processor, blend together the tofu,
cinnamon, vanilla, and maple syrup until smooth. Spoon into
a small bowl and use as a dip for the slices of apple and other
fruits. Makes approximately 1 1/2 cups.

*Erin's Comments: This dish is a delicious way to get some
calcium into your kids.*

Another great dip idea: Try apples and peanut butter, or
other nut butters. My toddler loves to dip everything, and
sometimes the easiest way to get her to eat an apple is to
put out some peanut butter to go with it.

Tamari Toasted Almonds

Compliments of Allison Rivers, President and Founder of Allison's Gourmet. www.allisonsgourmet.com

Ingredients:
- 2 cups raw almonds
- 1 to 2 tablespoons tamari

Directions:
Preheat oven to 350 degrees. Spread almonds in one layer on a baking sheet. Bake for 10-15 minutes or until almonds brown and smell toasty. Remove sheet pan from oven and sprinkle tamari over nuts and toss to coat evenly. Cool at least ten minutes and serve. After completely cooled (30 minutes or more) store in an airtight container at room temperature to stay fresh for up to one week.

Erin's Comments: Kids love these snacks and they are high in calcium!

For your information: Do you know the difference between soy sauce and tamari? Soy sauce contains wheat and preservatives. Tamari is of a higher quality and does not contain wheat.

DESSERTS

Festive Cashew Cookies
Reprinted with permission from Simply Vegan by Debra Wasserman
www.vrg.org

Ingredients:
- 2 cups raw cashews
- 1 cup rolled oats
- 1 teaspoon cinnamon
- 1/3 cup molasses or maple syrup
- 1/2 cup water
- 1/4 cup oil
- 1 teaspoon vanilla extract
- Small jar of unsweetened jam

Directions:
Preheat oven to 375 degrees. Grind the raw cashews and rolled oats together in a food processor for a few minutes. Pour mixture into a large bowl and add the remaining ingredients, except the jam. Mix all the ingredients together.

Form 24 round balls and place on a lightly oiled cookie sheet. With your thumb, form a small well in the center of each ball. Place a small amount of jam in each well.

Bake for 15 minutes at 375 degrees. Allow cookies to cool before removing them from the cookie sheet.

Erin's Comments: Young kids will enjoy using their thumbs to make the well in each cookie. Let them help put the jam in as well.

Peanut Butter Bars
Reprinted with permission from Cooking with PETA by PETA
www.peta.org

Ingredients:
- 6 cups corn flakes
- 1 cup light corn syrup
- 1 cup sugar or fructose
- 1 1/2 cups peanut butter
- 1 (8 oz.) bag non-dairy chocolate chips (or more depending on taste)

Directions:
Lightly oil an 8 x 10 inch cake pan, and place the corn flakes in the pan. Mix the corn syrup and sugar in a saucepan, and bring to a light boil. Remove from the heat, add the peanut butter, and mix until smooth. Pour the mixture over the corn flakes, and combine. In a double boiler or saucepan, melt the chocolate chips and pour over the top of the cereal mixture. Place in the refrigerator overnight to harden. The next day, cut and serve.

Erin's Comments: Great for potlucks, sleepovers, play dates, or any day!

Raspberry Oat Bar Cookies

Reprinted with permission from Eat Your Veggies by Beverly Lynn Bennett. www.veganchef.com

Ingredients:

- 1 1/3 cups whole wheat pastry flour
- 1 teaspoon salt
- 6 cups quick cooking oats
- 1 cup canola oil
- 1 cup maple syrup
- 2 teaspoons almond extract
- 2 teaspoons vanilla
- 1 cup fruit juice sweetened raspberry jam

Directions:

In a large bowl, sift together flour and salt. Stir in oats. Drizzle canola oil over the dry ingredients and toss well. Add maple syrup, almond extract, and vanilla, and thoroughly combine. Divide dough in half. Lightly grease a 9 x 13 inch pan. Using your fingers, firmly press half of the dough into the bottom of the greased pan. Carefully spread the raspberry jam over the entire surface of the dough. Sprinkle the remaining dough over the jam. Using your fingers, firmly press it to cover the jam, and pack it down tightly. Bake at 350 degrees for 30 – 40 minutes. Allow to cool before cutting into 24 squares.

Apple Pie
Recipe by Erin Pavlina

Ingredients:
- Pastry for two crust pie (following this recipe)
- 3/4 cup fructose or sugar
- 2 tablespoons whole-wheat pastry flour
- 1 teaspoon ground cinnamon
- 1/4 teaspoon ground nutmeg
- 1 to 2 teaspoons lemon juice
- 6 to 7 cups thinly sliced, peeled and cored cooking apples (2 lbs.)
- 1 tablespoon margarine
- Soymilk (for glazing)

Directions:
Put bottom crust in bottom of 9 inch pie plate.

In a small bowl, combine sugar, flour, cinnamon, nutmeg and lemon juice. Place half of thinly sliced apples in pie crust, sprinkle with half of sugar mixture. Top with rest of apples, then rest of sugar mixture. Dot the filling with margarine. Preheat oven to 425 degrees.

Roll out remaining crust. Cut out a design using a knife or cookie cutter (i.e. four small leaves). Place crust over pie; trim edges.

Fold pastry overhang under then bring up over pie plate rim. Pinch to form a high edge then make your choice of decorative edge. For golden glaze, brush the top crust (not the edge) lightly with some soymilk. Bake pie for 40-50 minutes or until crust is golden.

Pie Crust
Recipe by Erin Pavlina

Ingredients:
- 3 cups whole wheat pastry flour
- 1 teaspoon salt
- 3/4 cup margarine
- 5 to 6 tablespoons cold water

Directions:
In a medium bowl with fork, lightly stir together flour and salt. With pastry blender or two knives used scissor fashion, cut in margarine until mixture resembles coarse crumbs. Sprinkle in cold water, a tablespoon at a time, mixing lightly with a fork after each addition, until pastry just holds together.

With hands, shape pastry into ball (if it's a hot day you may have to refrigerate the dough for 30 minutes). For a two crust pie, divide pastry into 2 pieces, one slightly larger, and then gently shape each piece into a ball.

On lightly floured surface with lightly floured rolling pin, roll larger ball into a 1/8 inch thick circle, 2 inches larger all around than the pie plate. Roll half of circle onto rolling pin; transfer pastry to pie plate and unroll, easing into bottom and side of plate. Fill as recipe directs.

For top crust, roll smaller ball as for bottom crust; with sharp knife, cut a few slashes or a design in center of circle; center over filling in the bottom crust.

Fold overhang under; pinch a high edge. Bake pie as recipe directs.

Chocolate Peanut Butter Cups

Reprinted with permission from How It All Vegan!: Irresistible Recipes
for an Animal-Free Diet by Tanya Barnard and Sarah Kramer
www.GoVegan.net

Ingredients:
- 1/2 cup margarine
- 3/4 cup peanut butter or other nut butter (e.g. cashew)
- 3/4 cup graham wafer crumbs
- 1/4 cup dry sweetener
- 1 cup chocolate or carob chips
- 1/4 cup soymilk
- 1/4 cup nuts, chopped
- 12 cupcake paper liners

Directions:
In a small saucepan on medium heat, melt the margarine.
Once liquefied, stir in the peanut butter, graham crumbs, and
sweetener until well incorporated. Spoon about 2
tablespoons of the peanut mixture into muffin tins line with
cupcake paper lines (the liners are important.) In a different
small saucepan on medium heat, melt the chocolate and milk
together until completely melted, stirring often. Spoon over
top of the peanut butter cups. Garnish with nuts and allow to
set in the fridge for 6-8 hours before serving. Makes 12.

Chocolate Cake
Recipe by Erin Pavlina

Ingredients:
- 2 cups all-purpose flour
- 1 3/4 cups sugar or fructose
- 3/4 cup cocoa
- 1 1/4 cups soymilk
- 3/4 cup soy margarine
- 3 Ener-G Egg Replacer eggs (4 1/2 teaspoons egg replacer mixed with 6 tablespoons water)
- 1 1/4 teaspoons baking soda
- 1 teaspoon salt
- 1 teaspoon vanilla extract
- 1/2 teaspoon double-acting baking powder

Directions:
Preheat oven to 350 degrees. Grease and flour two 9-inch round cake pans or one 9 x 13 inch pan.

Into a large bowl, measure all ingredients. With mixer at low speed, beat until well mixed, constantly scraping bowl; at high speed, beat 5 minutes, scraping the bowl occasionally.

Pour into pan(s). Bake for 30 to 35 minutes or until done. Cool in pan on wire rack for 10 minutes, then flip it out of the pan upside down and cool completely on wire rack. Frost as desired.

Variation: You can make cupcakes instead, baking for 20 minutes instead. You can also add non-dairy chocolate chips to the batter before pouring it into the pan. See frosting recipes on next page.

Vegan Butter-Cream Frosting
Recipe by Erin Pavlina

Ingredients:
- 1 - 16oz. package confectioner's sugar (or make your own)
- 6 tablespoons margarine, softened
- 3 to 4 tablespoons soymilk
- 1 1/2 teaspoons vanilla extract
- 1/8 teaspoon salt

Directions:
In a large bowl with spoon or mixer at medium speed, beat all ingredients until very smooth, adding more soymilk if necessary to make the frosting a good spreading consistency.

Fudge Frosting
Recipe by Erin Pavlina

Ingredients:
- 2 cups non-dairy chocolate chips
- 1/4 cup soy margarine
- 3 cups confectioner's sugar
- ½ cup soymilk

Directions:
In a double boiler, over hot, not boiling, water, melt chocolate pieces with margarine. Stir in sugar and soymilk; remove from heat. With spoon, beat until smooth.

Resources

In an effort to provide you with the most current, up-to-date resources for living a vegan lifestyle and raising vegan children, following is a list of links on the VegFamily Web site that are updated frequently and guaranteed to be accurate.

Books (parenting, veganism, cookbooks, health, nutrition):
- www.vegfamily.com/books/index.htm

Vegan Products (reviews and a list):
- www.vegfamily.com/product-reviews/index.htm

Animal Ingredients List:
- www.vegfamily.com/lists/animal-ingredients.htm

Cruelty-Free Companies (companies offering cruelty-free products):
- www.vegfamily.com/lists/cruelty-free-companies.htm

Vegan Candy List
- www.vegfamily.com/lists/vegan-candy.htm

Veg-Friendly Playgroups
- www.vegfamily.com/playgroups/index.htm

Vegan Recipes
- www.vegfamily.com/vegan-recipes/index.htm

Articles (health, pregnancy, raising children, and teens)
- www.vegfamily.com/articles/index.htm
- www.vegfamily.com/vegan-pregnancy/index.htm
- www.vegfamily.com/babies-and-toddlers/index.htm
- www.vegfamily.com/vegan-children/index.htm
- www.vegfamily.com/vegan-teens/index.htm

Discussion Forums (chat with other parents raising vegan children)
- www.vegfamily.com/forums

References

Chapter 1: Becoming Vegan

Davis, Brenda, R.D., and Vesanto Melina, R.D., M.S. *Becoming Vegan*. Summertown: Book Publishing Company, 2000.

Marcus, Erik. *Vegan: The New Ethics of Eating*. Ithaca: McBooks Press, 1998.

Physicians Committee for Responsible Medicine. "New Four Food Groups Guidelines." *Vegetarian Starter Kit* 1999: 8-9.

Robbins, John. *Diet For a New America*. Walpole: StillPoint Publishing, 1987.

Stepaniak, Joanne, M.S., E.D. *The Vegan Sourcebook*. Los Angeles: Lowell House, 1998.

Chapter 3: Health

Mendelsohn, Robert S., M.D. *How to Raise a Healthy Child in Spite of Your Doctor*. New York: Ballantine Books, 1984.

Physicians Committee for Responsible Medicine. "Vegetarian Diets: Right From the Start." *Vegetarian Starter Kit* 1999: 10-12.

Physicians Committee for Responsible Medicine. "Vegetarian Diets: Advantages for Children." 12 June 2002. <http://www.pcrm.org/health/Info_on_Veg_Diets/vegetarian_kids.html>.

Physicians Committee for Responsible Medicine. "Vegetarian Foods: Powerful for Health." 13 June 2002. <http://www.pcrm.org/health/Info_on_Veg_Diets/vegetarian_foods.html>.

Vegetarian Resource Group. "Position of the American Dietetic Association: Vegetarian Diets." 13 June 2002. <http://www.vrg.org/nutrition/adapaper.htm>.

Chapter 4: Feeding Vegan Children

Davis, Brenda, R.D., and Vesanto Melina, R.D., M.S. *Becoming Vegan.* Summertown: Book Publishing Company, 2000.

PETA. "Vegan Children: Happy and Healthy."   14 June 2002. <http://www.peta.org/mc/facts/fsveg6.html>.

Stepaniak, Joanne, M.S., E.D. *The Vegan Sourcebook.* Los Angeles: Lowell House, 1998.

Vegetarian Resource Group. "Feeding Vegan Kids."   14 June 2002. <http://www.vrg.org/nutshell/kids.htm>.

Vegetarian Resource Group. "Feeding Vegan Children: Toddlers through School-Age."   14   June   2002.   <http://www.vrg.org/nutrition/pregnancy.htm>.

Vegetarian Society. "Information Sheet on Vitamin B_{12}." 17 June 2002. <http://www.vegsoc.org/info/b12.html>.

Vegetarian Society. "Information Sheet on Calcium."   17 June 2002. <http://www.vegsoc.org/info/calcium.html>.

Vegetarian Society. "Information Sheet on Vegan Nutrition."   17 June 2002. <http://www.vegsoc.org/info/vegan-nutrition.html>.

Walsh, Stephen, Ph.D. "What Every Vegan Should Know About Vitamin B_{12}."   *VegFamily.* 19   June   2002.   <http://www.vegfamily.com/articles/b12.htm>.

Chapter 5. Schools and Daycare

National Anti-Vivisection Society. "The Dissection Alternative Loan Program."   2   July   2002.   <http://www.navs.org/education/dissection_loan_program.cfm?SectionID=Education>.

Organic Consumers Association. "Vegetarian School Lunches are Hard to Find."   7 July 2002. <http://www.organicconsumers.org/school/news/veglunch.cfm>.

Physicians Committee for Responsible Medicine. "School Lunches Fail to Make the Grade, Say Doctors." 7 July 2002. <http://www.pcrm.org/news/health010904.html>.

Physicians Committee for Responsible Medicine. "Dissection Alternatives." 2 July 2002. <http://www.pcrm.org/issues/Animal_Experimentation_Issues/dissection_alternatives.html>.

Smith-Heavenrich, Sue. "Kids Hurting Kids: Bullies in the Schoolyard." *Mothering*. May/June 2001.

Wax, Emily. "Got Soy? Not in School Lunch." *Washington Post* April 14, 2002: A01.

Chapter 7: Traveling

Vegetarian Resource Group. "Traveling with Vegan Children." 16 July 2002. <http://www.vrg.org/journal/vj97may/976trav.htm>.

Chapter 8: Compassion in Action

Newkirk, Ingrid. *Kids Can Save the Animals: 101 Easy Things to Do.* New York: Warner Books, 1991.

"Ways to help the Environment." 29 July 2002. <http://library.thinkquest.org/11353/gather/help.htm>.

Chapter 9: Kid-Friendly Recipes

Selected recipes were re-printed with permission from the authors and/or publishers of the following cookbooks:

- *Simply Vegan* by Debra Wasserman. Vegetarian Resource Group, 1995.
- *The Compassionate Cook* by PETA and Ingrid Newkirk. Warner Books, 1993.
- *Cooking With PETA* by PETA. Book Publishing Company, 1997.

- *How It All Vegan* by Tanya Barnard and Sarah Kramer. Arsenal Pulp Press, 1999.
- *Eat Your Veggies* by Beverly Lynn Bennett. www.veganchef.com.
- *Incredibly Delicious: The Vegan Paradigm Cookbook* by Gentle World Publishing. Gentle World, 2000.
- Allison Rivers, Founder of Allison's Gourmet. www.allisonsgourmet.com. Delicious organic vegan cookies!

If you liked the information in this book, you'll love the FREE online magazine!

Visit www.VegFamily.com every month for new articles and information, and chat with other people raising vegan children.

Sign up for our FREE newsletter at www.VegFamily.com/newsletter.htm

If you would like to order **Raising Vegan Children in a Non-Vegan World** for yourself or as a gift, please visit:

www.vegfamily.com/bookstore/

If your group or organization would like to buy **Raising Vegan Children in a Non-Vegan World** in bulk at a discount, or for wholesale inquiries, please email:

info@vegfamily.com

Thank You For Reading!